100 LITERACY HOMEWORK ACTIVITIES

Published by Scholastic Ltd,
Villiers House,
Clarendon Avenue,
Leamington Spa,
Warwickshire CV32 5PR

4 5 6 7 8 9   5 6 7 8 9 0

AUTHORS
Kathleen Taylor, Wendy Jolliffe and David Waugh
EDITORIAL & DESIGN
Crystal Presentations Ltd
COVER DESIGN
Joy Monkhouse
COVER ARTWORK
Adrian Barclay
ILLUSTRATOR
Theresa Tibbetts

British Library Cataloguing-in-Publication Data
A catalogue record of this book is available from the British Library.

ISBN 0-439-01833-1

The publishers gratefully acknowledge permission to reproduce the following copyright material:

Colin and Jacqui Hawkins and **Dorling Kindersley** for the use of illustrations and text from *Tog the Dog* from the boxed set called *Pat the Cat and Friends* by Colin and Jacqui Hawkins (ISBN: 0-7513-5356-6) © 1988, Colin and Jacqui Hawkins (1995, Dorling Kindersley).

The Controller of HMSO and the DfEE for the use of extracts from *The National Literacy Strategy: Framework for Teaching* © 1998, Crown Copyright (1998, DfEE, Her Majesty's Stationery Office).

Macmillan Children's Books for the use of text and one illustration on page 53 from *Peace at Last* by Jill Murphy © 1982, Jill Murphy (1982, Macmillan). Five illustrations from page 53 and one illustration from page 41 copied with the approval of Jill Murphy by Lynda Murray and first appeared in *Read and Respond: Peace at Last* by Hilary Braund and Deborah Campbell © 1999, Scholastic Ltd (1999, Scholastic Ltd).

Mallinson Rendell Publishers Ltd, New Zealand for the use of text and illustrations from *Slinky Malinki* by Lynley Dodd © 1990, Lynley Dodd (1990, Mallinson Rendell Publishers Ltd).

Judith Nicholls for the use of 'Time for... ?' by Judith Nicholls from *Clock Poems* compiled by John Foster © 1993, Judith Nicholls (1993, OUP).

Every effort has been made to trace copyright holders. The publishers apologise for any inadvertent omissions.

CONTENTS

100 LITERACY HOMEWORK ACTIVITIES

About the series

100 Literacy Homework Activities is a series of teacher resource books for Years 1–6. Each book is year-specific and provides a core of word-, sentence- and text-level activities within the guidelines for the National Literacy Strategy in England. The content of these activities is also appropriate for and adaptable to the requirements of Primary 1–7 in Scottish schools.

Each book offers three terms of homework activities, matched to the termly planning in the National Literacy Strategy *Framework for Teaching* for that year. Schools in England and Wales that decide not to adopt the National Literacy Strategy will still find the objectives, approaches, content and lesson contexts familiar and valuable. However, the teacher will need to choose from the activities to match specific requirements and planning.

The homework activities provided in the books are intended as a support for the teacher, school literacy co-ordinator or trainee teacher. The series can be used alongside its companion series, *100 Literacy Hours,* or with any scheme of work, as the basis for planning homework activities throughout the school, in line with the school's homework policy. The resources are suitable for use with single or mixed-age classes, single- and mixed-ability groups and for team planning of homework across a year or stage. The teacher may also find the activities valuable for extension work in class or as additional resources for assessment. The teacher can even combine them to create a 'module' – a sequence of lessons on a common skill or theme, for example, by bringing together all the resource sheets on rhymes and rhyming words.

Using the books

The activities in each book are organised by term, then by word-, sentence- and text-level focus and, finally by specific National Literacy Strategy objective. Each of the 100 homework activities is comprised of at least one photocopiable page to send home. Each sheet provides instructions for the child and a brief note to the helper (be that a parent, grandparent, neighbour or sibling), stating simply and clearly its purpose and suggesting support and/or a further challenge to offer the child. Every sheet is clearly marked with a W (word), S (sentence) or T (text) symbol to designate its main focus. (Please note that 'they', 'them', 'their' has sometimes been used in the helper and teachers' notes to refer to 'child'. This avoids the 'he or she' construction.)

Some of the pages are designed for writing on; others are not. In the case of the latter – or when children wish to extend their writing – tell them to use the back of the page or a separate piece of paper. If appropriate, extra paper should be given out with the homework activity.

There is a supporting teachers' note for each activity. These notes include:

- **Objective:** the specific learning objective of the homework (referenced to the National Literacy Strategy *Framework for Teaching*).
- **Lesson context:** a brief description of the classroom experience recommended for the children prior to undertaking the homework.
- **Setting the homework:** advice on how to explain the work to the children and set it in context before it is taken home.
- **Differentiation:** where appropriate, advice on how to support the less able and challenge the more able. Most of the resource sheets have been designed with differentiation in mind and it is recommended that the teacher writes appropriate modifications to the general instructions on the reverse of the sheet. Occasionally, a homework sheet is aimed at a particular ability range and in these cases, suggestions for other children are given in the teachers' notes.
- **Back at school:** suggestions on how to respond to the returned homework, such as discussion with the children or specific advice on marking.

Making the most of these resources

The best way to use these homework resources is to use them flexibly, integrating them with a sequence of literacy sessions over a number of days. Such an approach will also ensure that the needs of an individual or groups of children are met in different ways. Some of the homework sheets will be greatly enhanced by enlarging to A3 size as this provides children with more space in which to write. Others, for example, the sets of story cards, lend themselves to being laminated for re-use.

Here are some ideas for different types of use:

Preparation

- Give a word- or sentence-level homework to prepare for a skills session later in the week. This allows the skill to be reviewed in less time, thus leaving more time for group activities.
- Give a text-level homework as a way of preparing for more detailed work on a particular type of text in a future literacy lesson.
- Give work on a particular short text as a preparation for further work on that text or a related text in a future lesson.

Follow-up

- Give a word- or sentence-level homework as a follow-up to a literacy lesson to provide more practice in a particular skill.
- Give a text-level homework as a creative way of responding to work done in a literacy lesson.
- Use one of the many short texts as a follow-up to a study of a similar type of text in a lesson.

Reinforcement

- Give a carefully selected word- or sentence-level homework to specific children who need extra practice.
- Give a text-level homework to specific children to reinforce text-level work done in class.
- Use a short text with specific children to reinforce work done on similar texts.

Supporting your helpers

The importance of involving parents in homework is generally acknowledged. For this reason, as well as the 'Dear Helper' note on each homework sheet, there is also a homework diary sheet on page 128 which can be photocopied and sent home with the homework. Multiple copies of these can be filed or stapled together to make a longer-term homework record. For each activity, there is space to record its title, the date on which it was sent home and spaces for responses to the work from the helper, the child and the teacher. The homework diary is intended to encourage home–school links, so that parents and carers know what is being taught and can make informed comments about their child's progress.

It is also worth writing to parents and helpers, or holding a meeting, to discuss their role. This could include an explanation of how they can support their children's homework, for example, by:

- providing an appropriate space where the child can concentrate and has the necessary resources to hand;
- becoming actively involved by interpreting instructions, helping with problems, sharing reading and participating in the paired activities where required.

Discuss with them how much time you expect the child to spend on the homework. If, after that time, a child is stuck, or has not finished, then suggest to the parent/helper that they should not force the child to continue. Ask them to write an explanation and the teacher will give extra help the next day. However, if children are succeeding at the task and need more time, this can be allowed – but bear in mind that children need a varied and balanced home life!

It is worth discussing with parents what is meant by 'help' as they should be careful that they do not go as far as doing the homework for the child. Legitimate help will include sharing the reading of texts, helping to clarify problems, discussing possible answers, etc., but it is important that the child is at some stage left to do his or her best. The teacher can then form an accurate assessment of the child's strengths and weaknesses and provide suitable follow-up work.

Using the activities with the 100 Literacy Hours series

A cross-referenced grid has been provided (on pages 6 and 7) for those who wish to use these homework activities with the corresponding *100 Literacy Hours* book. The grid suggests if and where a homework task might fit within the context of the appropriate *100 Literacy Hours* unit and there may be more than one appropriate activity. Note that, on some occasions, the best homework will be to continue or finish off the classwork, to read a text, to learn spellings, or to research a topic. Sometimes, the homework page could be used for a skills session in class and one of the resources from *100 Literacy Hours* can be used for homework.

UNITS IN 100 LITERACY HOURS: Y1			100 LITERACY HOMEWORK ACTIVITIES		
HOUR	PAGE	Term 1	Term 1	PAGE	NLS OBJECTIVE
		Unit	Title		
1	23	Hairy Maclary	Match the rhymes	28	W1
2	24		Slinky Malinki	51	T4
3	25		Capital letters hunt	45	S5
1	31	Zug the Bug	Make an og rhyme	29	W1
2	32		Full stop ahead!	46	S5
3	32		Tog the Dog	52	T4/W1
1	36	Where's Spot?	Dice words	32	W5
1	40	Have You Seen the Crocodile?	Crocodiles	34	W9
2	40		Have you seen the crocodile?	55	T6
1	46	Handa's Surprise	Describe the place	54	T5
2	46		Spell well (1)	38	W11
3	47		Hidden words	37	W10
4	48		Favourite fruit	49	T2
5	48		Fruity full stops	48	S8
1	54	The Little Red Hen	Colourful words	36	W9/11
2	55		The Little Red Hen: a picture story	50	T3
3	56		Can you help?	57	T9
4	57		What's wrong?	40	S2
5	58		The Little Red Hen	43	S4
1	63	Peace at Last	Change the word	33	W5
2	64		Mr Bear	41	S3
3	64		Peace at Last	53	T4
1	69	Another Day	Time for...?	56	T6
2	69		Spot the stop	47	S5
3	70		Number rhymes	30	W1
1	76	What's Cooking?	How to make a jungle scene	59	T13
2	77		My jungle scene	44	S4
3	78		Word wheel	31	W1
1	84	School Day	Spell well (2)	39	W11
2	85		School day	42	S4
3	86		Our school day	58	T12
4	86		A day at school	35	W9
5	87		Money for Monday	60	T15
		Term 2	Term 2		
1	92	The Three Little Pigs: Reading	Make a word	62	W3
2	92		Roll a word	63	W3/S1
3	93		The Three Billy Goats Gruff	81	T4
4	93		Spell well (3)	69	W9
5	94		What they might say	82	T4/5
1	101	The Three Little Pigs: Writing	Create-a-story game	85	T14
2	102		Likes and dislikes	73	S5
3	103		Rhyming pairs	61	W2
4	103		Rhyming story	77	T1
5	104		Beginnings and endings	83	T10
1	107	The Grass House	Guess the game	67	W7
1	112	A Busy Day	The Clever Cockerel & the Crafty Fox	74	S5
2	112		Pick a position	70	W9/S1
3	113		Be a poet	84	T13
1	119	Bear Hunt	Sh, sh, sh!	71	W10
2	120		What's the story	86	T16
3	120		Pick a pair	65	W3

UNITS IN 100 LITERACY HOURS: Y1			100 LITERACY HOMEWORK ACTIVITIES		
HOUR	PAGE	Term 2	Term 2	PAGE	NLS OBJECTIVE
		Unit	Title		
4	121		A place poem	72	S1
5	122		Letter sounds	64	W3
1	125	Little Bear	Two Little Bears	76	S7
2	125		How would you feel?	75	S5/6
3	126		Sort the rhymes	68	W7
4	126		Book covers	80	T3
5	127		Little Samantha's day	78	T2
1	132	Say Cheese!	Making a fruit salad	93	T23
2	132		Slide a word	66	W3
3	133		Chocolate charmer	79	T2
1	137	Information Books	Fiction or non-fiction?	87	T17/19
2	138		Label the house	92	T22
3	138		Indexes	89	T20
4	139		Questions, questions	94	T24
5	140		All about seeds	88	T18
1	143	Order! Order!	Order! Order!	90	T20
2	144		Using dictionaries	91	T20
		Term 3			
1	150	Polar Bear, Polar Bear	Adding 'ing'	102	W6
2	150		Adding 'ed' or 'd'	104	W6
3	151		The Bear's Just Had Twins!	114	T2
4	152		The Polar Bear and the Hobyahs	115	T5/6
5	153		Animal sounds and actions	103	W6
1	162	Non-fiction: Polar Bears	Question or not?	113	S7
2	162		Sequence	122	T18
3	163		Jumbled words	108	S2
4	164		Favourite animals	123	T19
5	165		My day at school	125	T20
1	168	Mister Magnolia	Sort the sound	95	W1
2	169		Word slide	97	W1
3	170		Phoneme sounds (1)	96	W1
1	172	Mr McGee Goes to Sea	Long vowel sounds (1)	98	W1
2	172		Long vowel sounds (2)	99	W1
1	177	Cats	Ill in bed	109	S4
2	177		Create an animal poem	121	T16
3	178		Pussy Cat, Pussy Cat	100	W1
1	182	I Wonder	Ask a question	127	T22
2	182		Missing vowels	107	W9
3	183		Create a poem	120	T16
1	187	The Little Box	Tell a story, write a story	119	T14
2	187		Spell well (4)	106	W7
1	193	Funnybones	Phoneme sounds (2)	101	W1
2	194		Sentence to punctuate	111	S6
1	199	Alex and Roy	What sort of story?	117	T7
2	200		Capital letters	110	S5
3	200		What's happening?	118	T13
4	201		What happens next?	116	T5
5	202		Match words to pictures	105	W6
1	206	Locating Information	My dad	124	T19
2	206		What is Dad thinking?	112	S6
3	207		What I know about my mum	126	T21

Teachers' notes

TERM 1

p28 MATCH THE RHYMES

Objective
Explore and play with rhyming patterns. (Y1, T1, W1)

Lesson context
Any lesson in which oral work on rhyming patterns has been carried out and children are able to match pairs of rhyming sounds. This homework would follow on well from having read in class the story, *Slinky Malinki* by Lynley Dodd (Puffin, ISBN 0-14-054449-9).

Setting the homework
Explain to the children that they should look carefully at the word and picture cards, and ask their helper for help with reading the words. They will then need to match the rhyming words and pictures.

Differentiation
There may be a few children whose phonological awareness has not sufficiently developed to be able to match rhyming sounds. However, practice at carrying out this activity, with a helper repeating the sounds, should help develop sound discrimination.

Back at school
As a quick assessment, ask the children to put the pictures on their tables in front of them and carry out a 'show me' type activity, with the children showing you the picture that rhymes with 'pegs', etc. (You could enlarge one copy, as teachers' 'show me' cards.)

p29 MAKE AN OG RHYME

Objective
Generate rhyming strings. (Y1, T1, W1)

Lesson context
Any lesson which contained demonstration and practice of onset and rime, for example using magnetic letters.

Setting the homework
Ensure the children understand that they need to make real words ending in the letters *-og*. If necessary, demonstrate using another letter string, such as *-at* or *-ig*.

Differentiation
Children will need to be familiar with all initial phonemes to carry out this activity. Those children who are not sure will need more support from helpers to look at each letter and say the sound.

Back at school
Ask different children to demonstrate to the class the words they have made, possibly by using magnetic letters, with the alphabet set out at the top and the rime underneath.

p30 NUMBER RHYMES

Objective
Generate rhyming words. (Y1, T1, W1)

Lesson context
Any lesson which has included an activity generating rhymes for words, particularly number words.

Setting the homework
Explain to the children that they are going to think of words to rhyme with the numbers one to five. The pictures are there to start them off.

Differentiation
Children will need to have a sufficient level of phonological awareness to recognise, discriminate and then generate rhymes. A few children may, therefore, need further support.

Back at school
Ask different children to read out the number rhyming words they found. You could display these with the numbers in the classroom.

p31 WORD WHEEL

Objective
Generate rhyming strings. (Y1, T1, W1)

Lesson context
Word-level activities using word wheels, after whole-class demonstration.

Setting the homework
Ensure that the children understand how a word wheel works. They should have previous experience with word wheels in the classroom. Photocopying the sheet onto card will help the durability. If you feel it is appropriate, you could make up the wheels *before* sending them home.

Differentiation
Children will need to be able to identify the phonemes on the wheel. Those who are not sure will require additional support.

Back at school
Ask children to demonstrate the different words they made.

p32 DICE WORDS

Objective
Blend phonemes to read CVC words. (Y1, T1, W5)

Lesson context
Any lesson which has contained demonstration of blending CVC words.

Setting the homework
Make up the dice and show the children how to make a word by throwing first a consonant, then a vowel and finally another consonant. Say each phoneme and then demonstrate blending the sounds together.

Differentiation
This activity is appropriate for those children who are able to identify all initial phonemes. Children who are not able to do so will require plenty of support to carry out this activity.

Back at school
Ask one or two children to demonstrate making words using the dice.

p33 CHANGE THE WORD

Objective
Blend letters in CVC words. (Y1, T1, W5)

Lesson context
Whole class or group work carrying out a similar activity blending CVC words.

Setting the homework
Ensure that children realise they need to place a different vowel letter in between the consonants to make different words. Tell them that the letters *b* and *h* should be tried instead of the *p*. They are not to be used in the middle.

Differentiation
This activity is suitable for children who can identify all vowel letters and make the short vowel sound. They will also need to know some consonant phonemes. Children who are not confident of this will need plenty of support.

Back at school
Play the game in class and ask different children to read the words that are made.

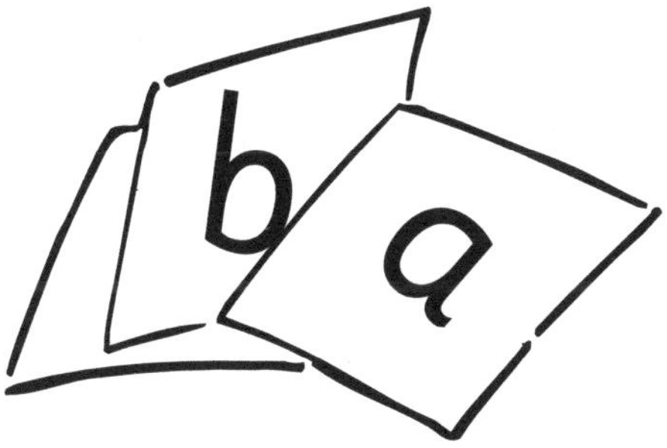

p34 CROCODILES

Objective
Track high-frequency words when reading. (Y1, T1, W9)

Lesson context
Any lesson where you have demonstrated tracking for words by scanning carefully through an extract of text together for a specific word. This would also fit well with a lesson using non-fiction.

Setting the homework
Explain to the children that they are going to look for key words in an information text about crocodiles, just as you have practised in class.

Back at school
Enlarge the text and words and ask one or two children to show the class how many times they can find each word.

p35 A DAY AT SCHOOL

Objective
Read on sight high-frequency words. (Y1, T1, W9)

Lesson context
Any lesson where you have demonstrated tracking for words by scanning carefully through an extract of text together for a specific word.

Setting the homework
Explain to the children that they are going to look for key words in the extract about school, just as you have practised in class.

Back at school
Enlarge the text and words and ask one or two children to show the class how many times they can find each word.

p36 COLOURFUL WORDS

Objectives
Read on sight and spell high-frequency words.
(Y1, T1, W9/11)

Lesson context
Any lesson which has been reinforcing high-frequency words. This would also follow on from handwriting practice sessions.

Setting the homework
Explain to the children that they will need to use different coloured crayons to write each word several times. Stress the importance of always starting at the right place (where the dot is) and following the right direction.

Back at school
Ask children to write the words as you dictate them. If you have small whiteboards, children can hold up each word to show you.

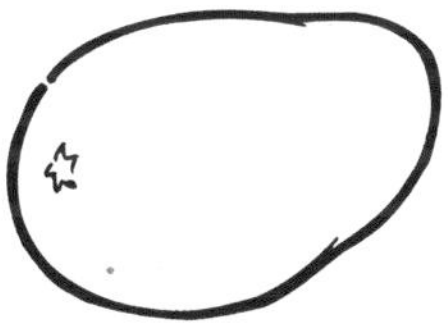

p37 HIDDEN WORDS

Objective
Recognise the critical features of words. (Y1, T1, W10)

Lesson context
Word-level work, looking at critical features of words and finding words hidden within words, eg 'the' in 'then'. This could form part of a shared reading session, using a text which refers to different fruit, such as *Handa's Surprise* by Eileen Browne (Walker, ISBN 0-7445-3660-X).

Setting the homework
Explain to the children that they will need to look closely at the letters in the words 'pineapple' and 'mango' and see how many words they can find, eg 'man' and 'go'. They could then go on to use all the letters jumbled up to make words. (Answers include: Pineapple - pine, apple, pin, pal, pale, pail, peal, peel, pile, pip, pie, pan, in, nip, nap, nail, eel, lap, lip. Mango - man, go, an, ago, no, on.)

Back at school
Ask children to talk about words they have found and write a list on the board.

p38/p39 SPELL WELL (1) & (2)

Objective
Spell common irregular words. (Y1, T1, W11)

Lesson context
Spelling activities during word-level work investigating ways of learning irregular words, eg mnemonics (for 'said' – Sally Ann Is Dizzy).

Setting the homework
Ensure that children are used to the 'Look-say-cover-write-check' routine of learning spellings.

Differentiation
You may wish to restrict the number of words for less able children, or add more for the more able.

Back at school
Carry out a spelling test to see if the children have learned the words.

p40 WHAT'S WRONG?

Objective
Use awareness of grammar to check if a sentence makes sense. (Y1, T1, S2)

Lesson context
This activity could follow on from reading in class the story of *The Little Red Hen*, particularly if you have substituted words that are not grammatically correct for the children to find the mistakes. This is an effective way of reinforcing the use of syntactical cues for reading.

Setting the homework
Explain to the children that they are going to be the teacher and mark the mistakes. You might read the first sentence to emphasise that it does not make sense.

Back at school
Re-read the incorrect story and ask children to suggest corrections. You could enlarge the text to do so.

p41 MR BEAR

Objective
Use grammatical awareness to read with expression. (Y1, T1, S3)

Lesson context
Any lesson where children have had the opportunity to take part in shared reading of a story with different voices to emphasise expression. This would ideally follow on from work on the story of *Peace at Last* by Jill Murphy (Macmillan, ISBN 0-333-63198-6).

Setting the homework
Explain to the children that they should practise reading the extract with their helper to make it sound like Mr Bear is really cross!

Differentiation
Less able children will need to have the helper read the extract with them, joining in where possible.

Back at school
Select one or two children to read the extract to the class.

p42 SCHOOL DAY

Objective
Match correct captions to pictures. (Y1, T1, S4)

Lesson context
Any lesson which has involved practice in matching words to pictures.

Setting the homework
Explain to the children that they need to read the sentences and find which picture matches.

Differentiation
Less able children will need helpers to read the sentences with them.

Back at school
Enlarge the pictures and sentences and ask children to show which match.

p43 THE LITTLE RED HEN

Objective
Write captions and simple sentences. (Y1, T1, S4)

Lesson context
This should follow on from work on the story of *The Little Red Hen*.

Setting the homework
Explain to the children that they need to write sentences to match the pictures. Point out that there are words provided to help them.

Differentiation
All children should be encouraged to attempt writing. For those lacking in confidence or ability, ask helpers to scribe parts for them.

Back at school
Encourage children to read their sentences to the class and display the results in the classroom.

p44 MY JUNGLE SCENE

Objective
Write a caption. (Y1, T1, S4)

Lesson context
Any lesson which has involved the children in writing a caption for a picture they have drawn.

Setting the homework
Please note that this activity works with that on page 59 and is dependent on the children having completed it first. Explain to the children that they are going to write sentences to describe the jungle scene that they assembled for a previous homework. Ensure that the children have their previous work of a jungle scene to take home with them.

Differentiation
All children should be encouraged to attempt writing. For those lacking in confidence or ability, ask helpers to scribe parts for them.

Back at school
Ask selected children to show their drawings and read out their sentences. Display the results.

p45 CAPITAL LETTERS HUNT

Objective
Identify capital letters in names. (Y1, T1, S5)

Lesson context
Any lesson focussing on identifying capital letters used for names. It would be an ideal follow-up to reading the story *Slinky Malinki* by Lynley Dodd (Puffin, ISBN 0-14-054449-9).

Setting the homework
Explain to the children that they are going on a hunt – to find capital letters for names. They are going to read a bit of *Slinky Malinki*, then put a ring around every capital letter that begins someone's name.

Back at school
Display the extract (enlarged) and ask different children to underline all the names and then put a ring round the first letter of each name.

p46 FULL STOP AHEAD!

Objective
Recognise full stops when reading and name them. (Y1, T1, S5)

Lesson context
Any lesson where identifying full stops was the objective. Ideally this would follow from reading the story of *Tog the Dog* by Colin and Jacqui Hawkins (available from Dorling Kindersley Family Library as part of a boxed set called *Pat the Cat and Friends*, ISBN 0-7513-5356-6).

Setting the homework
Explain to the children that they should read the story and pause when there is a full stop. Then, they should put a ring round each full stop.

Differentiation
Less able children will need support from their helper to read the text.

Back at school
Using an enlarged extract, read it with the children pausing as appropriate. Select a child to put a ring round the full stops.

p47 SPOT THE STOPS!

Objective
Recognise full stops and capital letters when reading. (Y1, T1, S5)

Lesson context
Any lesson where identifying full stops was the objective.

Setting the homework
Explain to the children that they should read the extract and put a ring round the full stops.

Differentiation
Less able children will need support from their helper to read the text.

Back at school
Ask selected children to read out sentences they have written.

p48 FRUITY FULL STOPS

Objective
Use full stops to demarcate sentences. (Y1, T1, S8)

Lesson context
Any lesson which has demonstrated writing sentences and putting full stops in. Ideally, this would follow from reading the children's book, *Handa's Surprise* by Eileen Browne (Walker, ISBN 0-7445-3660-X).

Setting the homework
Remind the children that sentences begin with a capital letter and end with a full stop.

Back at school
Examine the children's work and display examples.

p49 FAVOURITE FRUIT

Objective
Read unfamiliar words by using context and pictures cues. (Y1, T1, T2)

Lesson context
Any lesson where you have demonstrated in shared reading using picture cues or context cues (by reading on or reading back) to work out an unknown word. Ideally, this would follow from reading *Handa's Surprise* by Eileen Browne (Walker, ISBN 0-7445-3660-X).

Setting the homework
Explain to the children that they will need to look carefully at the pictures and words to answer the questions.

Differentiation
Less able children will need support from a helper to answer the questions.

Back at school
Ask different children to read out answers to the questions.

p50 THE LITTLE RED HEN: A PICTURE STORY

Objective
Re-tell a well known story. (Y1, T1, T3)

Lesson context
This activity should follow on from reading the story of *The Little Red Hen*. Experience of re-telling stories using story language should be regularly reinforced.

Setting the homework
Explain to the children that they need to look carefully at the pictures and tell the story to a helper.

Back at school
Select different children to re-tell the story to the class.

p51 SLINKY MALINKI

Objective
Make correspondence between words said and read. (Y1, T1, T4)

Lesson context
Any shared reading lesson where you have demonstrated one-to-one correspondence of spoken to written word by using a pointer to point to the words as you read, as well as reading the text looking for specific words (which you have written on card or on the board). It would be an ideal follow-up to reading the story *Slinky Malinki* by Lynley Dodd (Puffin, ISBN 0-14-054449-9).

Setting the homework
Explain to the children that they will read an extract from *Slinky Malinki* with a helper and then they will need to re-read looking for the particular words given.

Differentiation
Less able children will need support from a helper to read the story.

Back at school
Display an enlarged copy of the extract. Randomly give out word cards to the children and, as you read the extract, ask each one in turn to hold up their card when they hear the corresponding word.

p52 TOG THE DOG

Objectives
Read a simple story independently; explore rhyming patterns. (Y1, T1, T4/W1)

Lesson context
Ideally, this would follow from reading the story *Tog the Dog* by Colin and Jacqui Hawkins (available from Dorling Kindersley Family Library as part of a boxed set called *Pat the Cat and Friends*, ISBN 0-7513-5356-6), or another rhyming text where you have demonstrated pausing for children to provide the rhyming word.

Setting the homework
Explain to the children that they will read a short story about *Tog the dog* with their helper and that they should look for the rhyming words.

Differentiation
Less able children will need support from a helper to read the story.

Back at school
Re-read the extract with the class, pausing for them to fill in the rhyming words.

p53 PEACE AT LAST

Objective
Sequence a story correctly. (Y1, T1, T4)

Lesson context
This activity could follow from reading the story of *Peace at Last* by Jill Murphy (Macmillan, ISBN 0-333-63198-6) and/or from experience of sequencing sections of a story.

Setting the homework
Explain to the children that they will need to put the pictures in the right order, after having heard the story read to them.

Differentiation
For less able children, ask their helper to read the story summary through several times to support their child's memory of the sequence.

Back at school
Ask selected children to explain to the rest of the class the correct order of the pictures.

p54 DESCRIBE THE PLACE

Objective
Describe story settings. (Y1, T1, T5)

Lesson context
Any lesson which has concentrated on describing a story setting.

Setting the homework
Explain to the children that they will need to look carefully at the pictures and read the descriptions. Then, they need to match them.

Differentiation
Less able children will need help in reading the descriptions.

Back at school
Ask children to show which description matched which picture.

p55 HAVE YOU SEEN THE CROCODILE?

Objective
Substitute words in a patterned text. (Y1, T1, T6)

Lesson context
Shared reading of the story *Have You Seen the Crocodile?* by Colin West (Walker, ISBN 0-7445-1065-1) or a similar patterned text.

Setting the homework
Explain to the children that they will need to look carefully at the pictures to see which animal words they need to write.

Differentiation
Less able children may need helpers to scribe the words.

Back at school
Examine carefully children's writing and display examples.

p56 TIME FOR...?

Objective
Predict rhyming words. (Y1, T1, T6)

Lesson context
Shared reading of any rhyming text where children are able to add or substitute suitable words.

Setting the homework
Explain to the children that they will read a poem with their helper and look for rhyming words.

Back at school
Re-read the poem with the class and pause for them to add the rhyming words.

p57 CAN YOU HELP?

Objective
Write simple sentences based on a familiar story. (Y1, T1, T9)

Lesson context
This could follow from shared reading of the story of *The Little Red Hen*, or any story where helping others is a theme.

Setting the homework
Explain to the children that they will need to look carefully at the pictures and then complete the sentences.

Differentiation
Less able children may need their helper to scribe the sentences for them.

Back at school
Ask selected children to share the sentences they have written.

p58 OUR SCHOOL DAY

Objective
Read captions. (Y1, T1, T12)

Lesson context
Shared reading of various captions to pictures.

Setting the homework
Explain to the children that they will need to look at the pictures about the school day and read the words with their helper. They then need to answer the questions.

Differentiation
Less able children may need their helper to scribe the sentences for them.

Back at school
Ask selected children to read out the answers they have written.

p59 HOW TO MAKE A JUNGLE SCENE

Objective
Read and follow simple instructions. (Y1, T1, T13)

Lesson context
Any lesson that has involved reading and following instructions.

Setting the homework
Please note that this activity works with that on page 44. The children will have to have done this before doing page 44. Explain to the children that they will need to read and follow instructions to make a picture with a helper. It may be helpful to talk to the parents first to ensure that crayons, scissors and glue are available at home to do the activity.

Back at school
Ask children to share their completed pictures. If children are going to be undertaking the activity on page 44, ensure that the pictures are kept in a safe place as they will be needed for that activity.

p60 MONEY FOR MONDAY

Objective
Write a simple list. (Y1, T1, T15)

Lesson context
Shared writing of a list for a specific purpose.

Setting the homework
Explain to the children that they are going to write a list of things to remember for school each day. Make sure everyone knows what is needed on each day!

Differentiation
Less able children may need a helper to scribe for them.

Back at school
Discuss different lists and display them on the class notice board.

TERM 2

p61 RHYMING PAIRS

Objective
Investigate, read and spell words ending in *-ff*, *-ll*, *-ss*, *-ck* and *-ng*. (Y1, T2, W2)

Lesson context
Any lesson where word-level work focuses on word endings.

Setting the homework
Explain that the children will need help in cutting out and making the cards. Show the children a set of words you have already made and choose four children to demonstrate how to play the game. Tell them that their helper should play the game with them, but that once they have mastered the game, they could play it with other members of their family and friends.

Differentiation
All children should find the game fun to play. Some whose phonological awareness is not sufficiently developed will need to spend time in relating pronunciation to spelling. The more able could be directed to increasing the number of cards by adding other pairs of words with similar endings.

Back at school
Select children to read, say and spell some of the words from the game.

p62 MAKE A WORD

Objective
Read and spell words with initial consonant clusters. (Y1, T2, W3)

Lesson context
Any lesson which has contained a demonstration and practice of onset and rime. The homework would follow on well from having used the rhyming refrain in *The Three Little Pigs* as a lead into reading and spelling simple rhyming words.

Setting the homework
Explain to the children that they will need to ask their helper to assist with making the cards and with reading the words when the cards are turned over. Show them a set of words you have already made and choose two children to demonstrate how the game is played.

Differentiation
There may be a few children whose phonological awareness has not been developed sufficiently to be able to read and say the words; however, practice at carrying out the activity with the helper should help to develop reading and spelling skills.

Back at school
Ask different children to demonstrate using the cards to make words and read them.

p63 ROLL A WORD

Objectives
Read and spell words with initial consonant clusters; sort words for those that make sense and use them in a sentence. (Y1, T2, W3/S1)

Lesson context
Any lesson which has contained demonstration and practice of making new words using onset and rime and a discussion as to whether or not the words make sense.

Setting the homework
Explain to the children that they will need to ask their helper to assist with making the dice. Ask the children to discuss with their helper whether or not the word makes sense and how they would use it in a sentence. You may wish to demonstrate rolling the dice, making a word and using it in a sentence.

Differentiation
There may be some children for whom making words using onset and rime will be sufficient, whilst others will be capable of sorting words for sense and using them in a sentence.

Back at school
Ask different children to read out loud a sentence they have made up, and ask other children to guess which word in the sentence was made by rolling the dice.

p64 LETTER SOUNDS

Objective
Segment clusters of phonemes for spelling. (Y1, T2, W3)

Lesson context
Any whole-class, word-level work on phonemes.

Setting the homework
Remind the children about listening for the sounds of letters in words and tell them they are going to find the sounds in the list of words on the sheet by drawing a line between each sound. They should say each phoneme and then demonstrate they can blend the sounds together.

Differentiation
Children will need to identify the phonemes and, for those whose phonological awareness is less developed, greater assistance will be required from the helper.

Back at school
Ask one or two children to demonstrate segmenting words by phonemes, then blending the phonemes together into words.

p65 PICK A PAIR

Objective
Read and spell words with final consonant clusters. (Y1, T2, W3)

Lesson context
Any whole-class, word-level lesson where the focus has been on word endings, in particular final consonant clusters.

Setting the homework
Explain that the children will need help in cutting out the words and making them into cards. Remind the children of the importance of phoneme sounds in words in order to make them become better spellers and ask them to blend the sounds together if they encounter difficulty reading the words.

Differentiation
All the children will be able to play the game, but some will need greater assistance when blending phonemes together.

Back at school
Carry out a spelling test to see if children know the words.

p66 SLIDE A WORD

Objective
Discriminate, read and spell words with final consonant clusters *-tch*, *-nch*. (Y1, T2, W3)

Lesson context
Any whole-class word-level work demonstrating how to use word slides for final consonant clusters.

Setting the homework
Explain to the children that they will need their helper to help them cut out and make the word slides, and to use them to make words as demonstrated in the lesson.

Differentiation
All children should read and say the words they make. More able children could be asked to think of other words ending in *-tch* and *-nch* not on the slide.

Back at school
Carry out a spelling test to see if the children can spell the words.

p67 GUESS THE GAME

Objective
Investigate and spell words ending in *-s* and *-ss*. (Y1, T2, W7)

Lesson context
Any lesson where word-level work focuses on critical features of words, especially common spelling patterns of word endings.

Setting the homework
Explain to the children that they will need their helper to assist them in reading the passage and that they should predict the missing words and write them correctly in the text. Tell the children to rely on their own sight knowledge for the spellings of the common words 'yes' and 'was', and make informed guesses for other words which they should check for correctness with their helper.

Differentiation
The task is differentiated whereby children whose reading and spelling strategies are advanced will find fewer spellings over which to deliberate whereas other children of average and lower abilities will need to discuss with their helper whether the word should have *-s* or *-ss*.

Back at school
Ask children to offer spellings orally for a selection of other words ending in *-ss*, eg 'floss', 'moss', 'pass', 'miss'.

p68 SORT THE RHYMES

Objective
Recognise common spelling patterns within words. (Y1, T2, W7)

Lesson context
Any whole-class skills work where children are learning new words and making links to familiar spelling patterns.

Setting the homework
Explain to the children that they have to sort the rhyming words by their spellings.

Differentiation
The more able children should be directed to the additional activity of finding other spelling patterns for the rhyme.

Back at school
Make an enlarged grid for the classroom with columns marked *ear, air, ere, eir, are* to which children can add words as they find them during reading activities.

p69 SPELL WELL (3)

Objective
Learn to spell common irregular words. (Y1, T2, W9)

Lesson context
Spelling activities during word-level work investigating ways of learning irregular words. Ensure that children are used to the 'Look-say-cover-write-check' routine of learning spellings.

Setting the homework
Explain to the children that they will be using 'Look-say-cover-write-check' to learn to spell common words and that they will fold over the page to cover the words before they write them.

Differentiation
You may wish to restrict or add to the number of words. You may also restrict the sentence-level part of this work to your more able children.

Back at school
Carry out a spelling test to see if the children know the words. Ask some of the children who have used the words in sentences to read them out and ask other children to offer a meaning for the word.

p70 PICK A POSITION

Objectives
Spell high-frequency words; expect reading to make sense. (Y1, T2, W9/S1)

Lesson context
Any lesson where whole-class, word-level work focuses on the spelling of high-frequency words and/or where a shared reading session involves children in predicting masked words.

Setting the homework
Explain to the children that they need to use the pictures to help them predict the missing words.

Differentiation
Children who may encounter difficulty in reading the captions will need their helper to read the caption, leaving a gap for the child to predict the missing word.

Back at school
Carry out a spelling test to see if the children can spell the high-frequency words from memory.

p71 SH, SH, SH!

Objective
Read and spell a collection of words that contain the *sh* sound. (Y1, T2, W10)

Lesson context
A shared reading or guided reading session where text is tracked for the *sh* sound in order to find out where it occurs in words.

Setting the homework
Explain that the children are going to use the *sh* sound to complete the spelling of words which they should then read and use to make sentences.

Differentiation
More able children could make sentences for all the words, whereas average and lower-ability children might make fewer sentences, using only familiar words from the list. The children can use the back of their sheet to write more sentences.

Back at school
In guided reading sessions, check that children are using phonic/graphic knowledge to help them decode unfamiliar words containing the *sh* sound and spelling.

p72 A PLACE POEM

Objective
Read words and use in a sentence to make sense. (Y1, T2, S1)

Lesson context
A whole-class shared reading lesson where children are required to predict position words that have been masked out.

Setting the homework
Remind the children about position words. Tell them that they are going to use some position words to create a little poem, and explain how to follow the instructions on the homework sheet, reading out the example poem.

Differentiation
All the children should compose and write a poem. Some might be helped by talking about their ideas first and may require help with their writing.

Back at school
Organise children in groups or pairs so that they can read each other's poems.

p73 LIKES AND DISLIKES

Objective
Write in sentences and use full stops appropriately. (Y1, T2, S5)

Lesson context
Any whole-class shared writing lesson where sentence punctuation is the focus.

Setting the homework
Explain to the children that they have to complete the sentences by writing their views and opinions on the variety of subjects on the sheet. Remind them of the need to demarcate the end of a sentence by the use of a full stop.

Differentiation
More able children may wish to write further sentences on subjects of their choice.

Back at school
Check for any children who have written more than expected and enable them to share their views with the whole class. Ask pairs of children to swap each other's work to check that full stops have been used correctly.

p74 THE CLEVER COCKEREL AND THE CRAFTY FOX

Objective
Use capital letters and full stops correctly. (Y1, T2, S5)

Lesson context
Any lesson where the whole-class skills work has focused upon sentence construction and punctuation.

Setting the homework
Tell the children that the sentences on the sheet make up a story but that the capital letters and full stops are missing. It is their job to punctuate the sentences correctly.

Differentiation
Provide a smaller selection of the less complex sentences for the less able children.

Back at school
Organise the children to work in pairs checking each other's work for correct punctuation. Then, read the whole story aloud together.

p75 HOW WOULD YOU FEEL?

Objective
Demarcate a sentence. (Y1, T2, S5/6)

Lesson context
Any whole-class skills work involving capital letters and full stops and/or as a follow-up to text response work on characters' feelings.

Setting the homework
Explain to the children that they are going to write sentences to describe how they would feel if they were in the same situation as the characters in the pictures. Model an example sentence using either one of the pictures on the page or another of your own choosing. Remind the children to start their sentences with capital letters and end them with full stops.

Differentiation
All the children should attempt to describe how they would feel, but some will require greater assistance from their helper to compose the sentences.

Back at school
Organise the children in groups or pairs so that they can share each other's responses to the pictures and check their work for the correct use of capital letters and full stops.

p76 TWO LITTLE BEARS

Objective
Use capital letters for the start of sentences. (Y1, T2, S7)

Lesson context
Any whole-class skills work where using capital letters at the beginning of sentences is being taught.

Setting the homework
Explain that the children are going to read a story with their helper and put capital letters at the beginning of sentences.

Differentiation
Remind less able children that capital letters will follow a full stop. Encourage them to look for the full stops.

Back at school
Using an enlarged text similar to the homework page, read with the children and select individuals to change lower case letters to capitals where appropriate.

p77 RHYMING STORY

Objective
Reinforce and apply word-level skills through shared and guided reading. (Y1, T2, T1)

Lesson context
Any lesson involving reading and/or writing rhyming stories.

Setting the homework
Explain to the children that they will need to spend some time with their helper discussing what is happening in the pictures in order to determine the story. The children should use the rhyming endings to help them fit the captions to the pictures.

Differentiation
Some children will require the captions to be read for them in order that they can match them to the pictures.

Back at school
Ask one or two children to read the rhyming story to the class.

p78 LITTLE SAMANTHA'S DAY

Objective
Use phonological, contextual, grammatical and graphic knowledge to make sense of reading. (Y1, T2, T2)

Lesson context
Any whole-class shared reading lesson where children are engaged in making sense of what they read.

Setting the homework
Explain to the children that they have to re-order some sentences that rhyme in order to make a rhyming story.

Differentiation
Some children will need the sentences reading to them and greater assistance from their helper when putting them in sequence.

Back at school
Select children to read the rhyming story.

p79 CHOCOLATE CHARMER

Objective
Use phonological, contextual, grammatical and graphic knowledge to work out meanings of unfamiliar words. (Y1, T2, T2)

Lesson context
Whole-class shared reading of a recipe text.

Differentiation
All children should be able to use their reading skills to determine the appropriate word for the picture. Children will rely in varying degrees upon phonological, graphic, contextual and grammatical clues.

Back at school
Select children to talk about how they were able to read the new and unfamiliar words as a means of assessing their reading skills.

p80 BOOK COVERS

Objective
Predict what a story will be about from the cover and be able to discuss preferences, giving reasons why. (Y1, T2, T3)

Lesson context
Whole-class shared reading where a new book is being introduced.

Setting the homework
Explain to the children that it is important they should be able to talk about books, to be able to predict what a book might be about and to explain why they may prefer one book rather than another. Tell them they should talk to their helpers about what they think the books shown on the homework page might be about and whether or not they would like to read them.

Differentiation
Some children will need greater support from their helper when producing explanations and reasons for their preferences.

Back at school
In a whole-class shared reading lesson, show the children two different book covers and elicit a discussion in order that the children can practise their skills in speaking about what a book might be about and why they might like to read it.

p81 THE THREE BILLY GOATS GRUFF

Objective
Understand time and sequential relationships in stories, ie what happened when. (Y1, T2, T4)

Lesson context
As a follow-up to any reading or telling of a traditional tale.

Setting the homework
Explain to the children that their helper should read the story to them so that they can re-tell it back or to someone else.

Differentiation
Less able children will need greater assistance in the form of prompting when re-telling the story whereas more able children should be able to make links between different events in the story and answer questions such as: *What happened when Big Billy Goat Gruff crossed the bridge?*

Back at school
Ask the children a number of questions which draw from the children their ability to make links between the events in the story.

p82 WHAT THEY MIGHT SAY

Objectives
Give the main points of a story in sequence, and use dialogue in re-telling the story. (Y1, T2, T4/5)

Lesson context
A whole-class shared reading lesson where emphasis is given to what characters say.

Setting the homework
Explain to the children that they have to read and then match the speech bubbles to the appropriate pictures and read the speech bubbles with appropriate expression.

Differentiation
Some children will need greater assistance in reading the dialogue in the speech bubbles in order to apply the appropriate expression. As a further activity for the more able children, suggest re-telling the whole story where child and helper play the different parts of the goats and the troll.

Back at school
Ask one or two children to re-tell the story of *The Three Billy Goats Gruff* using their homework page as a prompt.

p83 BEGINNINGS AND ENDINGS

Objective
Identify beginnings and endings of stories. (Y1, T2, T10)

Lesson context
This homework activity would support any shared story writing activity.

Setting the homework
Explain to the children the need to read each bit of text carefully with their helper and decide whether it would be best used for the beginning of a story or at the end.

Differentiation
Some children will need greater support in reading the beginnings and endings.

Back at school
Organise children into writing groups. Ask each group to choose a beginning and an ending and use them to write a group story.

p84 BE A POET

Objective
Substitute and extend patterns from reading introducing new words. (Y1, T2, T13)

Lesson context
A shared writing lesson where children are involved in extending rhymes or composing poems.

Setting the homework
Work through the process of describing a favourite sweet, using the example on the sheet and alerting children to the way in which the sound of some words (onomatopoeia) captures exactly a particular aspect of the sweet.

Differentiation
Some children will require their helper to suggest descriptive words from which the child could choose.

Back at school
As part of shared reading, discuss some of the poems with the class, asking children to explain why some words used to describe the chosen subjects are better than others. Display the poems where children and parents can easily read them.

p85 CREATE-A-STORY GAME

Objective
Write a story from a given plot structure. (Y1, T2, T14)

Lesson context
Any shared reading lesson where story plot is being discussed.

Setting the homework
Explain that this activity can involve the whole family where lots of funny stories can be created. Simply make more story strips. Briefly explain the process of folding over and passing on the strip.

Differentiation
Some children will need assistance in writing the responses.

Back at school
Ask one or two children to read aloud their funny stories to the class. If appropriate, relate the plot structure to a class story currently being read to the children.

p86 WHAT'S THE STORY?

Objective
Use elements of known stories to structure own writing. (Y1, T2, T16)

Lesson context
Any shared writing or guided writing lessons where children are engaged in composing a story.

Setting the homework
Tell the children that they are going to write an exciting story using the picture on the sheet to help them. Tell them that they should ask their helper to write some of the story for them in the same way you do in class lessons.

Differentiation
The level of helper support will vary according to the writing skills of the child.

Back at school
Provide an opportunity to read some of the stories and use appropriate ones for the whole-class shared writing sessions in order to extend the teaching of story structures.

p87 FICTION OR NON-FICTION?

Objectives
Use the term *fiction* and *non-fiction*, noting some of their differing features; to predict what a given book might be about by a brief look at the cover. (Y1, T2, T17/19)

Lesson context
Any lesson where you are investigating the differing features of fiction and non-fiction.

Setting the homework
Ensure that the children know the terms *fiction* and *non-fiction* and have some concept of their differences. Discuss what the sheet requires them to do, and encourage them to explain to their helper why they made their decisions.

Differentiation
All children should be encouraged to explain their decisions.

Back at school
Set up a display of fiction and non-fiction books and ask the children to label them.

p88 ALL ABOUT SEEDS

Objective
Read non-fiction for comprehension. (Y1, T2, T18)

Lesson context
Any shared or guided reading lesson where children are required to interpret a non-fiction text.

Setting the homework
Explain to the children that their helper should read *All about seeds* to them and then they should read it again with the helper before answering the questions. Encourage them, when answering the questions, to look for key words in the text rather than re-reading the whole text.

Differentiation
All the children should be able to discern the relevant information from having the text *All about seeds* read to them. Some may need help in completing their written answers.

Back at school
Use a simpler test for further comprehension work in small groups.

p89 INDEXES

Objective
Understand alphabetical organisation in texts. (Y1, T2, T20)

Lesson context
Whole-class shared reading or group activities using indexes.

Setting the homework
Explain to the children that they will be sorting words into alphabetical order for an index like the ones they have seen in information books.

Differentiation
All children will need support in reading new and unfamiliar words.

Back in school
Provide a group activity task where the children use indexes and thereby further their understanding.

p90 ORDER! ORDER!

Objective
Secure knowledge about alphabetical order. (Y1, T2, T20)

Lesson context
Shared reading and/or group activities where children are investigating alphabetical order.

Setting the homework
Remind the children of the need to use the second letter of the word as a means of ordering.

Differentiation
All the children should be able to order the words, although some may need help reading the more difficult words such as 'axe', 'fur', 'foam', 'oar' and others.

Back at school
Continue to establish routines whereby children refer to dictionaries confidently.

p91 USING DICTIONARIES

Objective
Use simple dictionaries and understand their alphabetical organisation. (Y1, T2, T20)

Lesson context
Any lesson, whole-class shared reading or guided reading activity, where children are shown how to use dictionaries.

Setting the homework
Equip children with simple dictionaries if they haven't a dictionary at home. Explain to the children that they are to find the meanings of the words on the homework sheet using the dictionary as they do in group activities and shared reading.

Differentiation
Some children who find writing difficult will need greater assistance when writing sentences.

Back at school
Extend dictionary work by giving pairs of children a dictionary from which to locate words which you call out. Select pairs of children to read out the meanings of the words found.

p92 LABEL THE HOUSE

Objective
Write labels for a drawing. (Y1, T2, T22)

Lesson context
Whole-class shared reading or writing where labels are featured.

Setting the homework
Explain to the children how to label a drawing using the example on the homework sheet.

Differentiation
All children should be able to use their reading skills to determine the appropriate word and use it as a label on the picture.

Back at school
Display a large picture related to a current topic and ask a group of children to label it. Ask other groups to label equipment or specific resources in the classroom.

p93 MAKING A FRUIT SALAD

Objective
Write a simple explanation in the form of a caption. (Y1, T2, T23)

Lesson context
Any shared reading or writing session involving instructional genres such as a recipe.

Setting the homework
Explain to the children that they are going to write the instructions for making a fruit salad by using the pictures on the homework sheet and using the helpful words to begin their sentences.

Differentiation
Some children will need their helper to support them when writing a sentence.

Back at school
Organise the children into groups so that they can read and compare each other's instructions.

p94 QUESTIONS, QUESTIONS

Objective
Write simple questions. (Y1, T2, T24)

Lesson context
Any shared reading lesson where children are required to glean information from a picture and/or are asked to write questions.

Setting the homework
Tell the children they are going to ask questions that can be answered by looking at the picture. Give an example: *How many children are riding scooters? Which shop is next to the butchers' shop?*

Differentiation
Some children will require their helper to write for them, but all children should be encouraged to attempt to write for themselves.

Back at school
Display an enlarged version of a picture of the house and share some of the questions that have already been made. Elicit further questions from the children which could be placed around the picture.

p95 SORT THE SOUND

Objective
Identify the common spelling pattern for the long vowel sound oo. (Y1, T3, W1)

Lesson context
Any lesson where word-level work focuses on long vowel sounds.

Setting the homework
Talk about words which include different spellings of the oo sound. Explain that the children are going to sort words according to the spelling of the oo sound.

Differentiation
All the children should find they can sort the different spellings. More able children could go on to track their reading books for the sound.

Back at school
Provide an enlarged version of the table in order to collect oo sounding words the children find when reading. At the end of a week investigate the collection of different spellings.

p96 PHONEME SOUNDS (1)

Objective
Segment words into phonemes for spelling. (Y1, T3, W1)

Lesson context
Any lesson where word-level work focuses on segmenting words for sounds or where there is a particular emphasis on long vowel sounds.

Setting the homework
Explain to the children that they will need to listen carefully to the sounds (phonemes) that make up the words. Use the word *phoneme*. If appropriate, remind or tell the children that the long vowel sound is the name of the letter.

Differentiation
This activity is appropriate for those children who are able to identify phonemes. Children who are not able to do so will require additional support.

Back at school
Provide a set of different words on the flip chart and choose children to segment them.

p97 WORD SLIDE

Objective
Read and spell words ending in *-ew* and *-ue*. (Y1, T3, W1)

Lesson context
Any lesson where the focus is on identifying *ew* and *ue* sounds and learning their spellings.

Setting the homework
Explain to the children that they will require help in making the word slides, and that they should learn the spellings.

Back at school
Ask some of the children to write and spell the words from the slides on a flip chart and others to check if they are right by using the word slide.

p98 LONG VOWEL SOUNDS (1)

Objective
Learn the common spelling patterns for the long vowel sound *ie*. (Y1, T3, W1)

Lesson context
Any lesson where word-level work focuses on long vowel sound *ie*.

Setting the homework
You will need to give the children coloured counters. Talk about the words that include different spellings of the *ie* sound. Explain that the children are going to sort words by using different coloured counters to cover the different spellings of the sound *ie*.

Differentiation
This activity is suitable for all the children who can identify phonemes. Children who are less able will need more adult support in identifying the spellings. An extension activity for the more able would be to collect words containing the sound *ie* from their reading books.

Back at school
Provide other word grids so that the children can play the game and develop their skills. Look for evidence of children learning these words through conducting a spelling test.

p99 LONG VOWEL SOUNDS (2)

Objective
Learn the common spelling patterns for the long vowel sound o. (Y1, T3, W1)

Lesson context
Any lesson where word-level work focuses on long vowel sound o.

Setting the homework
You will need to give the children coloured counters. Talk about the words which include different spellings of the o sound. Explain that the children are going to sort words by using different coloured counters to cover the different spellings of the sound o.

Differentiation
This activity is suitable for all the children who can identify phonemes. Children who are less able will need more adult support in identifying the spellings. An extension activity for the more able would be to collect words containing the sound o from their reading books.

Back at school
Track the text the children are using in guided reading sessions for the long vowel sound o.

p100 PUSSY CAT, PUSSY CAT

Objective
Learn the common spelling patterns for the long vowel sounds *ee* and *ai*. (Y1, T3, W1).

Lesson context
Any lesson where word-level work focuses on identifying and spelling long vowel sounds *ee* and *ai*.

Setting the homework
Tell the children to enjoy the poem. Explain that they are going to listen for the *ee* sound as in 'me', 'tea' and 'tree' and the *ai* sound as in 'train' and 'say' in order to make a collection of words containing those sounds which can then be sorted by the spelling patterns into the grids.

Differentiation
Some children will need greater assistance to identify the sounds. Others could collect words containing those sounds from their reading book.

Back at school
Display extended versions of the grids to include further spellings of the sounds, for example, *ey* as in 'key' and *a* as in 'make' and *ay* as in 'play' in order to extend the children's awareness of the different spelling patterns.

p101 PHONEME SOUNDS (2)

Objective
Segment words into phonemes for spelling. (Y1, T3, W1)

Lesson context
Any lesson where word-level work focuses on segmenting words for sounds.

Setting the homework
Explain to the children that they will need to listen carefully to the sounds that make up the word.

Differentiation
Some children who have difficulty identifying sounds will need more adult support.

Back at school
Carry out a spelling test containing some of the words from the homework activity.

p102 ADDING 'ING'

Objective
Investigate and learn spellings of verbs with *-ing* endings. (Y1, T3, W6)

Lesson context
Any lesson where word-level work focuses on words ending in *-ing*.

Setting the homework
Tell the children that they are required to explain the different things that happen to words when adding *-ing* and will need their helper to help them to read the sheet and write the explanation.

Differentiation
Encourage all children to attempt writing explanations, but some will need extra adult support for this element of the task.

Back at school
Ask children for their explanations in order to display in the classroom the various rules to which children can refer.

p103 ANIMAL SOUNDS AND ACTIONS

Objective
Investigate and learn spellings of verbs with *-ing* endings. (Y1, T3, W6)

Lesson context
Any lesson where the word level work focuses on words ending in *-ing*.

Setting the homework
Reinforce the need to think about the ways in which words change when adding *-ing* and to check spellings in a dictionary.

Back at school
Develop the spelling activity for those children who need further reinforcement by giving them other animals on which to carry out the same activity.

p104 ADDING 'ED' OR 'D'

Objective
Investigate and learn spellings of verbs with *-ed* endings. (Y1, T3, W6)

Lesson context
Any lesson where spellings are the specific skills focus or where the ending *-ed* is being considered in relation to the tense of a sentence or a section of story.

Setting the homework
Ensure children understand the difference between the present and past by giving a few examples in sentences. Use the words on the sheet if you wish.

Back at school
Reinforce the activity with a supporting activity whereby children compose sentences using the words.

p105 MATCH WORDS TO PICTURES

Objective
Investigate and learn to spell words ending in *-ing*. (Y1, T3, W6)

Lesson context
Any lesson where the word ending *-ing* is being explored.

Setting the homework
Explain to the children that they are to match words to pictures and to ask their helper to assist them when writing the sentences. You may wish to work through one of the words together as an example of what to do.

Differentiation
All children should be able to match words to pictures. Some will require their helpers to support them when writing sentences.

Back at school
Ask individual children to spell some of the words explaining any changes that have occurred to the root word.

p106 SPELL WELL (4)

Objective
Learn to spell common irregular words. (Y1, T3, W7)

Lesson context
Any lesson which reinforces 'Look–say–cover–write–check' strategies or in which investigating ways of learning to spell irregular words has taken place.

Setting the homework
Explain to the children that they will be using 'Look–say–cover–write–check' to learn to spell common words and that they will fold over the page to cover the words before they write them.

Differentiation
More able children could be given additional irregular words, for example from the high frequency List 1 in the NLS.

Back at school
Carry out a spelling test to see if children know the words.

p107 MISSING VOWELS

Objective
Use the terms 'vowel' and 'consonant' correctly. (Y1, T3, W9)

Lesson context
Any lesson where the focus is on the short vowel sounds *a, e, i, o, u*.

Setting the homework
Tell the children that they have been given the consonants in the words and that they should sound out the words in order to add the vowels.

Differentiation
The words are phonetically regular so all the children should be able to attempt the task.

Back at school
Using the homework words, ask the children to name whether the letter is a consonant or a vowel.

p108 JUMBLED WORDS

Objective
Re-order words to make sense. (Y1, T3, S2)

Lesson context
All lessons where sentence-level work focuses on sentence structure and the use of capital letters and full stops.

Setting the homework
Tell the children to spend time with their helper discussing the picture before attempting the jumbled sentences. Remind the children to use the capital letters to help them find the beginning of a sentence and full stops to help them find the end.

Differentiation
Some less able children will need extra help when reading the words in the jumbled sentences.

Back at school
Ask some less able children to discuss the picture, intervening where necessary. Ask some more able children to think of other sentences they could compose from the picture, which they should write on a flip chart for all the others to read.

p109 ILL IN BED

Objective
Re-order sentences so that a poem rhymes and makes sense. (Y1, T3, S4)

Lesson context
Any lesson where sentence-level work focuses on predicting rhyme endings.

Setting the homework
Discuss with the children what the poem is about and explain how they have to put sentences in the correct order and to use the rhyme endings to help them.

Back at school
With the children read the poem, omitting the rhyme ending in order that the children can offer the rhyming words. Ask one child to read the poem whilst others provide a 'still' of one of the scenes.

p110 CAPITAL LETTERS

Objective
Use capitalisation for personal titles, book titles etc. (Y1, T3, S5)

Lesson context
Any session on sentence-level work where attention is given to where and why capital letters are used.

Setting the homework
Tell the children that capital letters are missing from the four sentences on the sheet. They should read the sentences, then write them in the space provided with the capital letters in the right place.

Differentiation
All children should be able to do the task, although some will need extra support when reading the sentences.

Back at school
Provide a selection of names of teachers, staff and helpers in school without capital letters so that children can supply them. Recap on different uses of capital letters.

p111 SENTENCES TO PUNCTUATE

Objective
Reinforce knowledge about sentences. (Y1, T3, S6)

Lesson context
A session where you recap on the use of full stops, capital letters and question marks.

Setting the homework
Tell the children what the sentences are about (ie set the scene) and tell them about the punctuation features you want them to use.

Differentiation
The sentences are set in a context to enable children who find reading difficult to follow the thread of a story.

Back at school
Choose some of the children to read out the account with expression appropriate to asking questions.

p112 WHAT IS DAD THINKING?

Objective
Reinforce knowledge about what a sentence is. (Y1, T3, S6)

Lesson context
Sentence-level work and shared writing sessions involving the composition of a sentence.

Setting the homework
Tell the children that they should all attempt to write sentences that describe what Dad wants to do instead of working in the house.

Back at school
Ask children to take turns to read out their sentences.

p113 QUESTION OR NOT?

Objective
Add question marks to questions. (Y1, T3, S7)

Lesson context
Sentence-level work and shared writing sessions where attention is given to questions and how to punctuate them.

Setting the homework
Discuss with the children the different inflection and expression we use when asking a question and use examples to make the point: eg *We are going to the zoo.* (statement). *Are we going to the zoo?* (question). Explain to the children that they should read the sentences aloud in order to hear the questions.

Back at school
Provide further statements and questions on the flip chart ready for children to provide the correct punctuation.

p114 THE BEAR'S JUST HAD TWINS!

Objective
Use phonological, grammatical and contextual knowledge in order to work out and predict rhyme and make sense of what is read. (Y1, T3, T2)

Lesson context
Any shared reading sessions when using rhyming poems or stories.

Setting the homework
Tell the children that they can ask their helper to assist in the reading of the poem, but that they should try to predict the rhyme ending themselves.

Back at school
Choose some of the children to read the poem omitting the endings for others to guess.

p115 THE POLAR BEAR AND THE HOBYAHS

Objectives
Re-tell stories with expression and give the main points in sequence, picking out significant incidents. (Y1, T3, T5/6)

Lesson context
Any shared reading session where re-telling and reading with expression is the focus.

Setting the homework
Emphasise that the point of this homework is not to be able to read the story but to be able to listen to the story being read and then to re-tell it. All children should ask their helpers to read the story to them.

Back at school
Choose one or two children to re-tell the story. A more able child could write the main points of the story on a flip chart.

p116 WHAT HAPPENS NEXT?

Objective
Re-tell stories with expression and give the main points in sequence. (Y1, T3, T5)

Lesson context
A shared reading or writing session where significant incidents in a story are being discussed or written about.

Setting the homework
Remind the children of the two traditional tales *The Three Little Pigs* and *The Three Billy Goats Gruff* and the points in the stories that the two pictures depict. Explain to the children that they have to re-tell the whole story to their helper, and that some children will need their helpers to help them write what happens next.

Differentiation
All children should know the traditional stories in the pictures and be able to re-tell the story to others. The more difficult aspect of this homework task is to write what happens next and some children will need extra support from their helpers at this point.

Back at school
Organise the children into groups for re-tellings. In a class session choose some children to read out their story endings.

p117 WHAT SORT OF STORY?

Objective
Use book 'blurbs' in order to predict the context of the stories. (Y1, T3, T7)

Lesson context
Any shared reading session where the focus is on predicting the contents of a book by reading covers and blurbs.

Setting the homework
Ask the children to explain what 'blurbs' on books do and explain that their homework involves reading 'blurbs'. Tell the children that they will be expected to report back to the class on the discussions they have with their helpers about what sort of stories they think the books will be about from the 'blurbs'.

Differentiation
Children who are less confident with books will require increased support from their helper in the form of more questioning and prompting.

Back at school
Organise children into groups so that they can share their opinions about what the books might be about. Follow this up by trying the activity in a whole-class shared reading session with some books from your classroom library.

Sarah goes to stay for a holiday with her grand-parents who live in a big house. She thinks she will be on her own with only Grandma and Grandad to play with. Then Tom arrives. From then on her days become very exciting!

p118 WHAT'S HAPPENING?

Objective
Write about significant incidents from known stories. (Y1, T3, T13)

Lesson context
A shared reading or writing session where significant incidents in stories are being discussed and written about. Particularly appropriate following the reading of *Cinderella*.

Setting the homework
Tell the children that they should all attempt to do all that is required but tell the most able to write as much as they want to about what is happening in the picture. They may use a separate piece of paper for this.

Differentiation
The less able children should concentrate on re-telling the story whereas the more able should be encouraged to write as much as they can about the incident depicted in the picture.

Back at school
Organise for some children to re-tell a story to a younger child, possibly in another class. Discuss children's writing with the aim of making improvements.

p119 TELL A STORY, WRITE A STORY

Objective
Write a story using a simple setting. (Y1, T3, T14)

Lesson context
A shared reading or writing session where the focus is on story structure.

Setting the homework
Discuss the picture on the homework sheet with all the children and establish clearly for them the setting in which they are to base their stories.

Back at school
Organise the children into groups so that they can share their stories. Choose some children to read their stories to the class.

p120 CREATE A POEM

Objective
Compose own poetic sentences using carefully selected words and imagery. (Y1, T3, T16)

Lesson context
A shared reading or writing session where the focus is on the structure of a poem.

Setting the homework
Read through the instructions and models on the homework sheet with all the children. Ask two children to read the two exemplar poems aloud to the class.

Differentiation
Some of the more able children should be able to do this activity by themselves, whereas others will need to discuss the focus of their poem, at length, with their helper.

Back at school
Make time, possibly over a few days, for children to read aloud their poems to the rest of the class. A class anthology could be made.

p121 CREATE AN ANIMAL POEM

Objective
Compose a sentence that has a poetic quality. (Y1, T3, T16)

Lesson context
A shared writing lesson where the focus is to create a class poem or to elaborate an existing poem.

Setting the homework
Read through the instructions and model on the homework sheet with all the children, pointing out the illustration and words used to describe the caterpillar.

Back at school
Make a class anthology, for example: 'Class 1's Book of Animal Poems'.

caterpillars crawl creepily

p122 SEQUENCE

Objective
Read recounts and begin to recognise the generic structure. (Y1, T3, T18)

Lesson context
Any shared reading lesson where the focus is on reading a recount.

Setting the homework
Remind the children of the key words at the beginning of each sentence which will help them to detect the right order.

Back at school
Organise for someone to brush their teeth while another child reads the recount. Ask the children: *Has anything been left out in the written recount?*

p123 FAVOURITE ANIMALS

Objective
Locate parts of a chart that give particular information in order to answer questions. (Y1, T3, T19)

Lesson context
A shared reading session where children are engaged in extracting facts from a piece of information.

Setting the homework
Read through the homework sheet explaining to the children how to read the chart.

Differentiation
The chart is 'child friendly' and all children should attempt the homework. Some will require support when reading the questions.

Back at school
Display an empty version of the chart in order to determine the favourite animals of children in the class.

p124 MY DAD

Objective
Locate information on a chart. (Y1, T3, T19)

Lesson context
Any shared reading session using a chart for locating information.

Setting the homework
Explain to the children what the chart is about, and what they have to do.

Differentiation
All children should be able to use the chart to locate information, but some will need extra help in reading the sentences.

Back at school
Organise children in groups so that they can check each other's work.

p125 MY DAY AT SCHOOL

Objective
Write simple recounts. (Y1, T3, T20)

Lesson context
A shared writing or guided writing lesson where the focus is a recount text.

Setting the homework
Explain the homework sheet, telling the children to discuss their school day with their helper.

Differentiation
The writing frame and the familiar setting should allow most children to complete this task. Some children will need their helper to write for them.

Back at school
Organise the children in pairs so that they can compare their writing about their day at school.

p126 WHAT I KNOW ABOUT MY MUM

Objective
Use the language and features of non-fiction texts. (Y1, T3, T21)

Lesson context
A shared writing session where you are gathering information.

Setting the homework
The homework sheet is quite easy to follow, so a brief explanation is all that should be required. Be sensitive to children's varying home situations. If appropriate, adapt the sheet so the child is writing about someone else they know well.

Back at school
Discuss with the children the features of the language: for example, short rather than long descriptions.

p127 ASK A QUESTION

Objective
Write own questions. (Y1, T3, T22)

Lesson context
Any shared reading or writing lesson where children are required to elicit questions.

Setting the homework
Explain to the children that the point of the homework is to be able to ask questions rather than answer questions. Talk about why this is an important skill in that reading involves the reader asking questions as well as finding answers.

Back at school
Collect all the different questions the children have raised and display them on a large sheet in large print so that children can read them. Use the questions at a further shared reading or writing lesson.

Name:

Match the rhymes

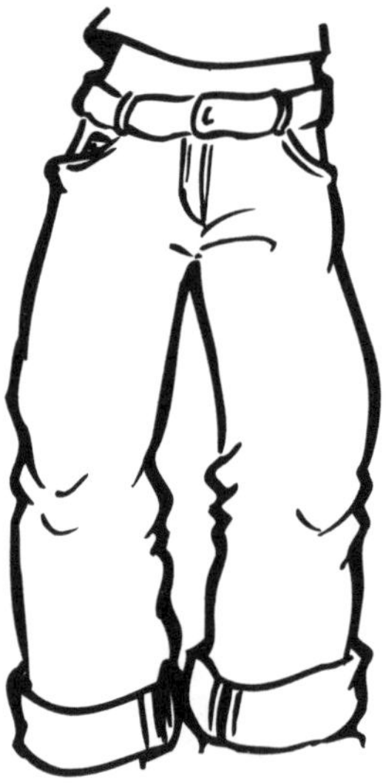
jeans

cat

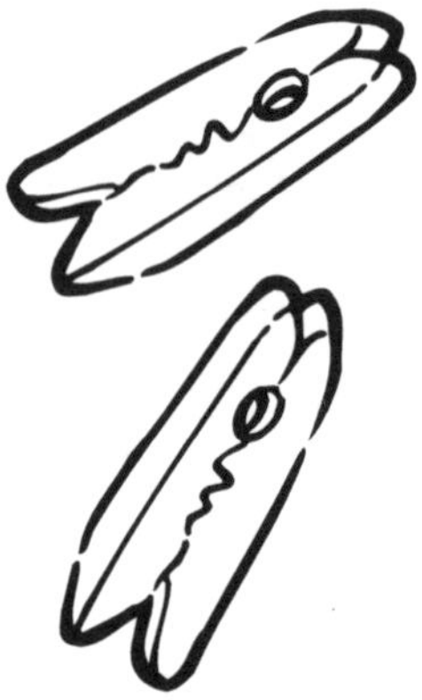
pegs

sock

clock

beans

legs

mat

- Cut up the pictures with the words underneath.
- Match the rhyming pictures.

Dear Helper,

Objective: to explore rhyming patterns.

After cutting out the pictures with the relevant words, spread the cards out. Look at each picture and read the word underneath. Explain that you need to put the words and pictures that rhyme together (eg *cat* and *mat*). When you have played this matching game several times, cut off the corresponding words and see if your child can match the rhyming words to the pictures. Move on to matching rhyming words on their own.

Name:

Make an og rhyme

- Try to put all the different letters in the alphabet in front of the letters below. How many words can you make?

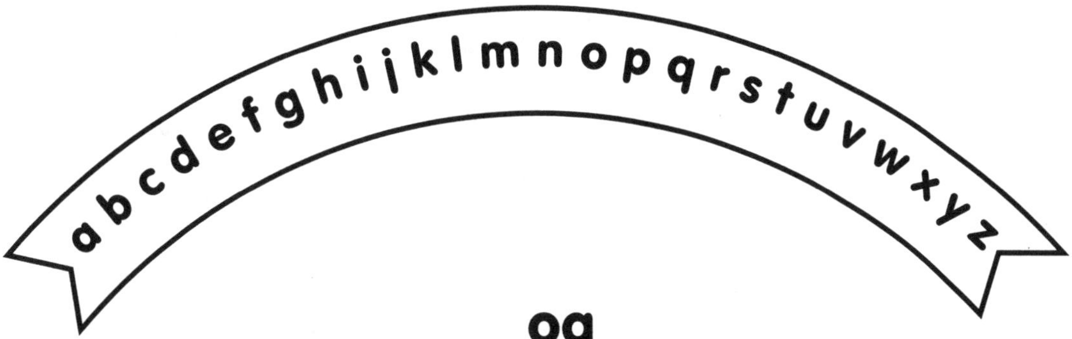

og

og

og

og

og

og

Dear Helper,

Objective: to make up rhyming words that share the same letter pattern.

Ask your child to see how many words they can make using different letters of the alphabet as the first letter and the ending -*og*. You can also try using two letters together (such as *fr*) and then adding -*og*. They can then write a list of the words they make. Can you make up a funny poem together?

PHOTOCOPIABLE

Name:

Number rhymes

- Look at the pictures of words that rhyme and say them.
- Think of other words that rhyme with each number.

one

two

three

four

five

Dear Helper,

Objective: to make up rhyming words.

Read the numbers and look at the corresponding rhyming pictures with your child. Say that you are going to make up words to rhyme with the numbers using the pictures to help. You can write a list of all the words that rhyme with each number and see if your child can think of any more.

Name:

Word wheel

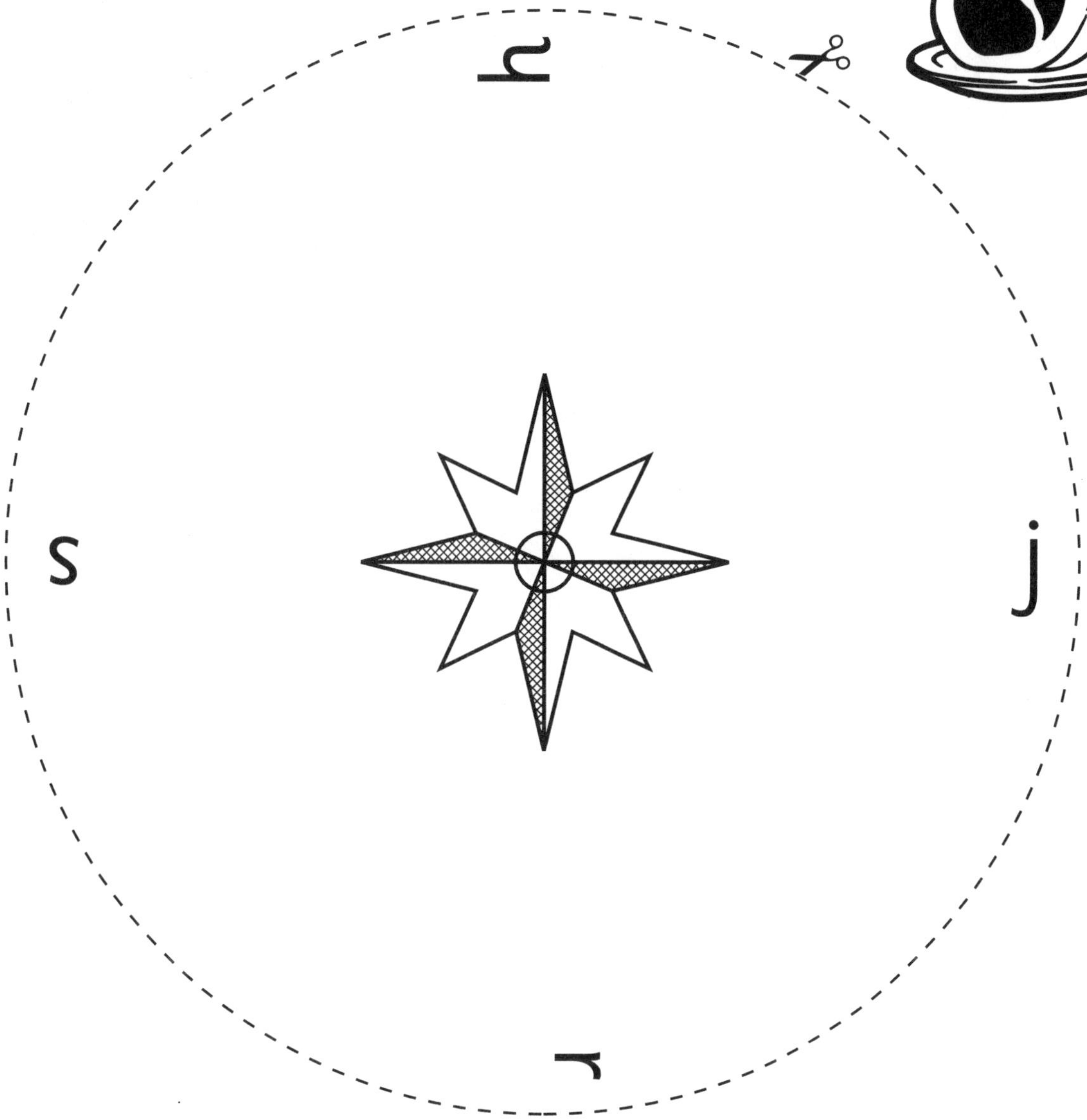

- Cut out the circle and the strip.
  Ask your helper to show you how to put them together.
- Turn the circle and see how many words you can make.

Dear Helper,

Objective: to read and make up words with *-am* ending.

Cut out the circular shape. If you stick this onto card it will make it stronger. Now cut out the strip containing the letters *am* and fix this behind the circle, using either a split pin, or a pencil. The letters *am* should just stick out from the circle. Now turn the circle and help your child to read the different words they make. Can they think of any other word beginnings to add to *-am* to make words, for example 'pram'?

PHOTOCOPIABLE

Name:

Dice words

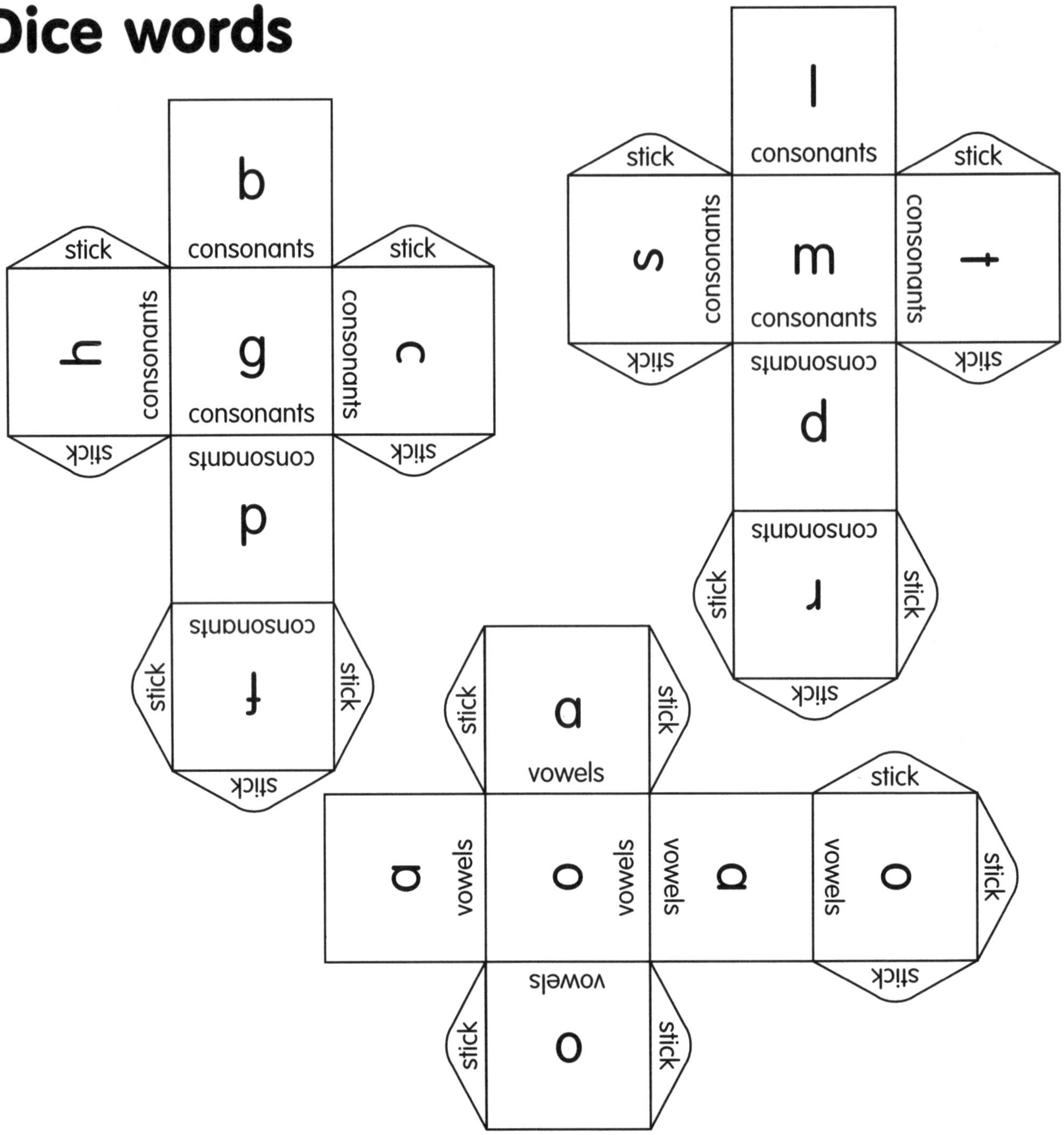

- Ask your helper to help you cut out the dice and stick them together.
- Throw a dice which has **consonants** on it. Now throw the dice with **vowels** and finally another **consonants** dice. Have you made a word?

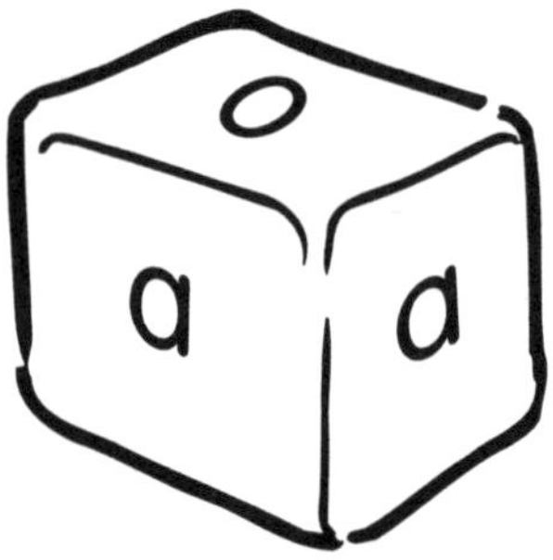

Dear Helper,

Objective: to blend three letters into a word.

You will need to make up the three dice, by cutting out and sticking together. If you can stick the paper dice onto card first, they will be stronger. Now play 'Dice words' with your child as described above. Ask your child to put the three letters next to each other and to say them aloud, blending them into a word. Ask: *Do they make a real word?* If so, write it on a list to take to school. Play again. How many different words can you and your child make?

Name:

W

Change the word

a	e	i
o	u	b
	h	

- Cut out the letters above.
- Place the vowels (**a**, **e**, **i**, **o** and **u**) in turn into the space between **p** and **t** below. How many words can you make?
- Now place the **b** over the **p** and play the game again. Play it again using the **h** instead of the **p**.

p		t

Dear Helper,

Objective: to blend three letters to read a word.

This is a game, where you need to cut out the vowel letters (*a*, *e*, *i* o, *u*) and ask your child to place one letter at a time in between the *p* and *t* to see which words they can make. Say the words each time with your child and encourage them to write a list of the words they make. The letters *b* and *h* have also been included for you to substitute with *p* to make further words.

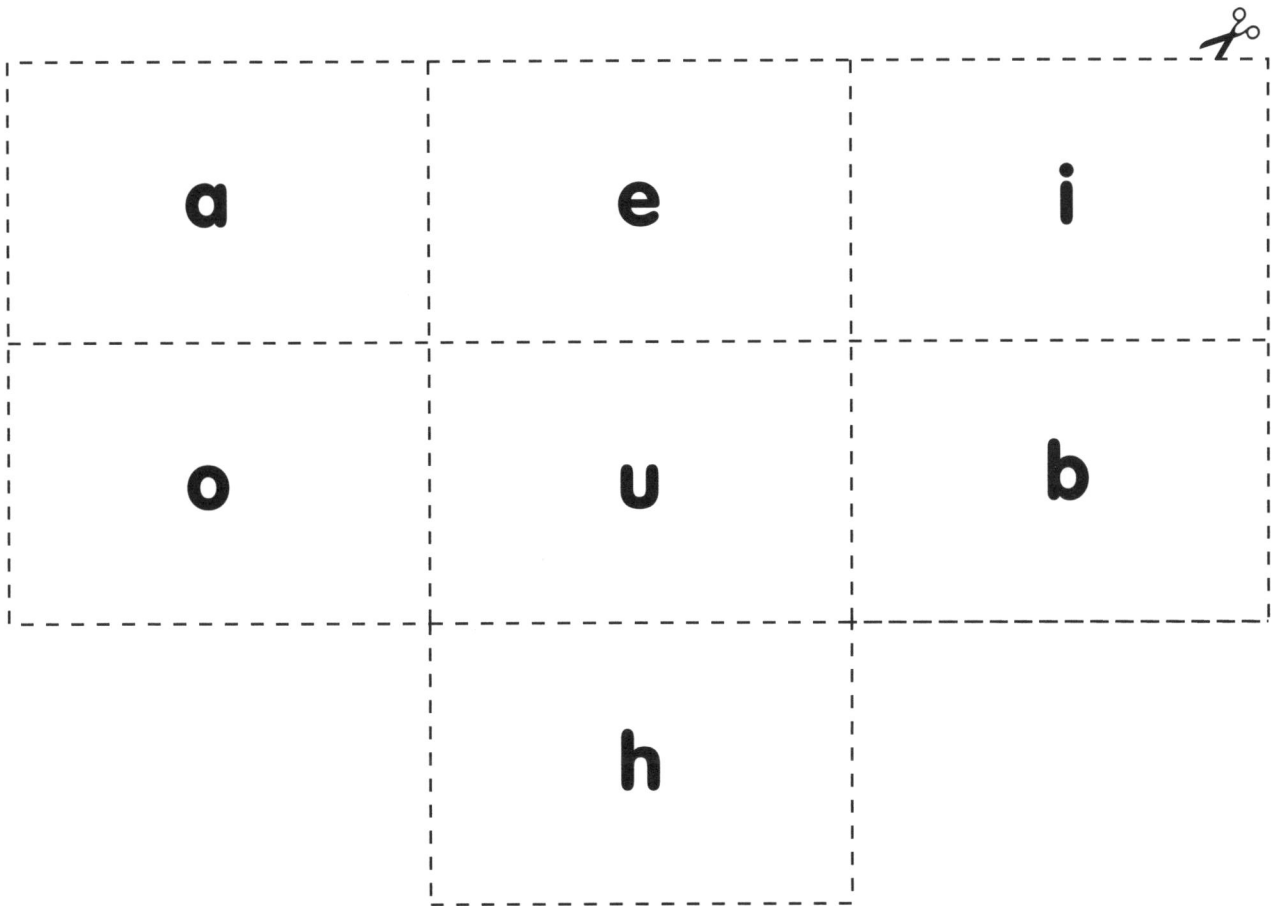

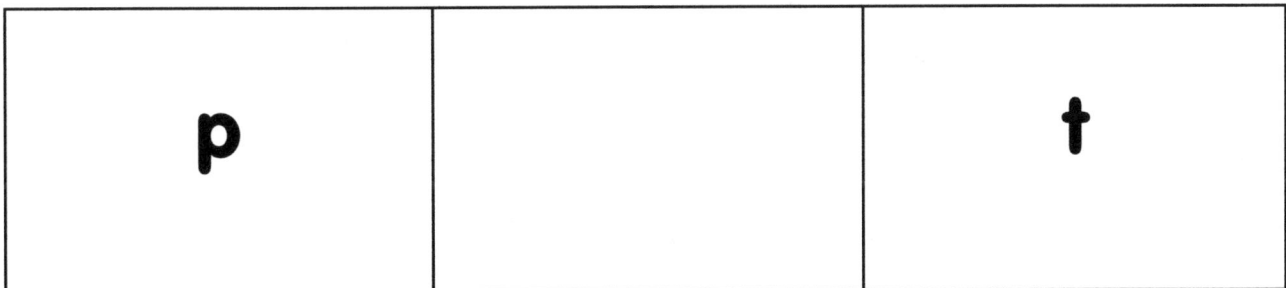

W Name:

Crocodiles

and	in	to	they

- Cut out the words above.
- Read about crocodiles with your helper, looking carefully for the words.

Crocodiles

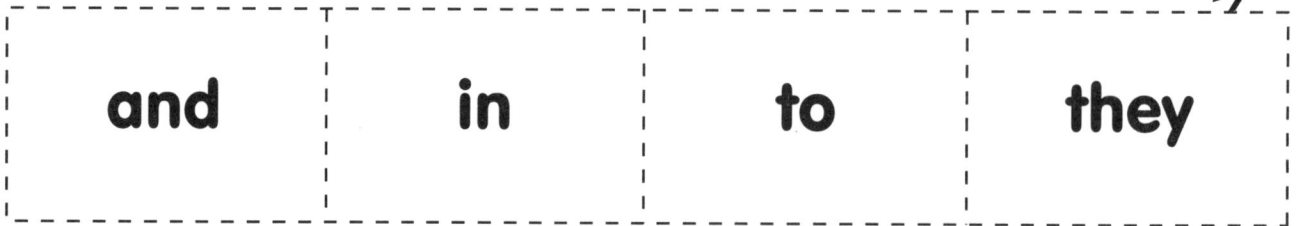

The crocodile hides in rivers and lakes and looks for something to eat. Crocodiles can eat frogs and fish whole and they catch larger animals by gripping them in their teeth and spinning round with them. They sometimes eat humans.

Female crocodiles lay eggs which they look after until they hatch. Tiny baby crocodiles listen for their mother's footsteps and call to her. She gently gathers them into her mouth and carries them to the safety of the water.

Dear Helper,

Objective: to identify common words in text.

Read the extract about crocodiles to your child and explain that it is giving them information about crocodiles (non-fiction). Now cut up the common words above and give your child one word at a time, asking them to search through the text for the same word. Your child should first say what the word says and then track their finger along the text until they find the corresponding word. You could provide coloured crayons to highlight the words, using a different colour for each word.

Name:

A day at school

it	**is**	**for**	**we**

- Cut out the words above.
- Read about 'A day at school'.
- Find the words you have cut out.

A day at school

The school day begins at 9 o'clock when the whistle blows and everyone has to line up in the playground. We line up in our classes and our teacher takes us into our cloakroom. As soon as we have hung up our coats and changed our shoes it is time for the register.

Next it is time for the reading. We read on the carpet with the teacher and learn the sounds that letters make. We have to work quietly at our tables. After we finish our work, we talk about it on the carpet and then it's soon time for assembly.

Playtime comes next. Children play chasing games and skipping. After playtime it is time for Maths. We have to listen carefully and hold up number cards to answer a question.

When Maths is finished it is time for lunch. Lots of children stay for school dinner. In the afternoon we have PE, Art, Music, Science and lots of other subjects. Last of all is a story before we go home.

Dear Helper,

Objective: to identify common words.

Read the text to your child, pointing to the words as you read. Cut up the common words at the top and give your child one word at a time, asking them to search through the text for the same word. Your child should first say what the word says and then track their finger along the text until they find the corresponding word. You could provide coloured crayons to highlight the words, using a different colour for each word.

PHOTOCOPIABLE

W Name:

Colourful words

- Practise writing over these words using different coloured crayons to help remember how to spell them and to improve your handwriting.

was	was	was
said	said	said
dog	dog	dog
cat	cat	cat

PHOTOCOPIABLE

Dear Helper,

Objective: to be able to read and write common words correctly.

Watch your child carefully as they form the letters. Make sure they start in the correct place for each letter. Ask them to say each letter (using the letter names) as they write it and then the whole word.

Name:

W

Hidden words

- There are words hidden inside these words.
  Look at the examples. How many more can you find?

pineapple

pine

mango

go

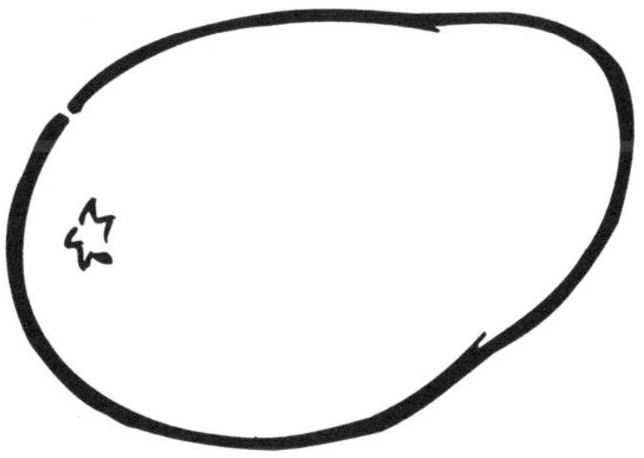

Dear Helper,

Objective: to find words within words.

Help your child to look carefully at the above words and see how many words they can find, such as *pine* in *pineapple*. Encourage them to use all the letters and see how many words they can make. Careful observation of letters in words is a good way to help your child with spelling. If you have any magnetic letters this would help. If not, write all the letters from each word on card or paper and cut out individually. Now your child can select from these letters to make different words with your help.

PHOTOCOPIABLE

W Name:

Spell well (1)

Remember!
Look at the word carefully.
Say the word aloud.
Cover the word while
you try to **write** the word.
Now **check** to see if it is right.

Look and Say	Cover	Write	Check
said			
was			
went			
play			
like			

PHOTOCOPIABLE

Dear Helper,

Objective: to learn to spell common words.

Help your child to spell these words by looking carefully at the letters in a word and saying the word aloud. Then, fold the paper so the word is covered. Now encourage them to try to write the word. Lastly, ask your child to check against the printed word.

Name:

Spell well (2)

Remember!
Look at the word carefully.
Say the word aloud.
Cover the word while
you try to **write** the word.
Now **check** to see if it is right.

Look and Say	Cover	Write	Check
for			
they			
going			
come			
my			

Dear Helper,

Objective: to learn to spell common words.

Help your child to spell these words by looking carefully at the letters in a word and saying the word aloud. Then, fold the paper so the word is covered. Now, encourage them to try to write the word. Lastly, ask your child to check against the printed word.

Name:

What's wrong?

- Read the story and draw a line under all the wrong words.

The Little Red Hen

Once upon a week there was a Little Red Hen who wanted to wheat some plant. She asked the cat, dog and pig to hop. They would not help. So she planted the water and waited for it to grow. She asked the cat, dig and pig to help cut the wheat but they would not hop. She cut it herself. She asked them to help grind the water but they would not hop. So she did it herself. They did not want to help her build the bread so she did it herself. They did want to hop eat the bread, but she did that all by themselves.

Dear Helper,

Objective: to use knowledge about correct words to check if sentences make sense.

Read the story with your child and see how many mistakes they spot. Re-read the story and ask your child to underline all the incorrect words.

Name:

Mr Bear

- Read the story and make Mr. Bear sound very cross!

Mr. Bear was tired
Mrs. Bear was tired
and
Baby Bear was tired...
...so they all went to bed.

Mrs. Bear fell asleep.
Mr. Bear didn't.

Mrs. Bear began to snore.
"SNORE," went Mrs. Bear,
"SNORE, SNORE, SNORE."
"Oh NO!" said Mr. Bear,
"I can't stand THIS."
So he got up and went to
sleep in Baby Bear's room.

Dear Helper,

Objective: to read with expression.

Read this extract first to your child, putting in as much expression as possible. Ask your child to try to read it with you. Then, ask your child to read it on their own using the correct expression.

Name:

School day

- Match the words to the pictures by writing the correct number under each picture.

1 The teacher calls the register.

2 We line up for assembly.

3 We all join in with singing.

4 We hold up number cards in Maths.

5 We read with our teacher.

6 We listen to a story before we go home.

Dear Helper,

Objective: to match captions to pictures.

Ask your child to read each caption and help if necessary. Then, match the captions to the appropriate pictures, putting a number underneath each picture.

Name:

The Little Red Hen

- Look at the pictures and write the story.

Words to help

Little Red Hen help dog cat pig plant bake bread

Who will help me plant this wheat?
Not I.

Once upon a time there was

Who will help me bake this bread?
Not I.

Who will help me eat this bread?
I will.

Dear Helper,

Objective: to write captions for pictures.

Help your child to write a sentence to fit each picture of the story of the Little Red Hen. You might explain that this represents the beginning, middle and end of the story.

Name:

My jungle scene

- Look at your jungle scene picture.
- Now write some sentences to describe it.

The tiger looks at ______________________________

____

The snake hisses at ____________________________

____

The monkey climbs the __________________________

____

The parrot's feathers are ________________________

____

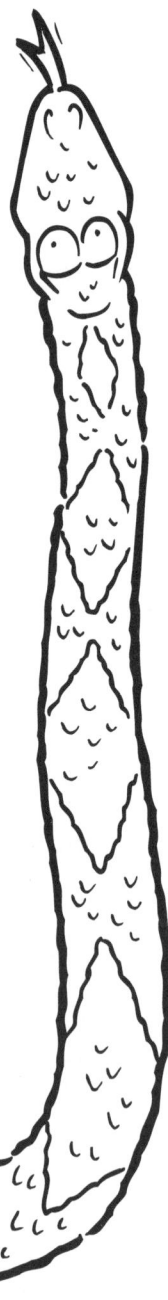

Words to help

trees	elephant	monkey	green
tiger	snake	red	yellow
parrot	small	blue	big

Dear Helper,

Objective: to write a caption.

Your child should look carefully at the picture of the jungle that they have constructed previously for homework. They should now complete the sentences above to describe it. They can use the words above to help them. Encourage your child to write more sentences if they are able.

Name:

Capital letters hunt

- Read part of the story of *Slinky Malinki*, the cat who was a burglar!
- Put a ring around all the capital letters for names.

Slinky Malinki

One rascally night
between midnight and four,
Slinky Malinki
stole MORE than before.
Some pegs and a teddy bear
dressed up in lace,
a gardening glove
from Macafferty's place.
A tatty old sneaker,
a smelly old sock
and Jennifer Turkington's
pottery smock.
A squishy banana,
some glue and a pen,
a cushion from
Oliver Tulliver's den.

Dear Helper,

Objective: to identify capital letters for names.

Read the above extract from *Slinky Malinki* by Lynley Dodd with your child. Talk about capital letters and say that one of the uses for capital letters is for people's names. Remind your child how to begin to write their own name. Give your child a pen or pencil and ask them to put a ring round every capital letter for someone's name. You can then help to write a list of all the names mentioned above.

Name:

Full stop ahead!

- Read the story of Tog.
- Find the full stops and put a ring around each one.

Tog the Dog

One day Tog the dog went out for a jog.
It was a very wet day and the path
was so muddy he fell into a bog.
Nearby was a big log and he managed
to pull himself out of the bog onto the log.
He was covered in mud and frightened a
frog sat by the bog. He had to jog all
the way home. Finally Tog the dog reached home
and sat on a log to dry.

Dear Helper,

Objective: to identify full stops and take account of them when reading.

Read the story of Tog with your child and encourage them to pause where there is a full stop. Ask your child to track carefully through the words and put rings round the full stops. Talk about using full stops to mark the end of sentences and how this helps to read a text and understand its meaning.

Name:

Spot the stops!

- Read the story.
- Look for all the full stops and put a ring round them.

Jonathon James could not get to sleep. He lay in his bed listening to the clock chime downtairs. He heard it chime eight times. Eight o'clock. He heard the music on the television which meant that his favourite programme had just finished. He had been sent to bed early for arguing and fighting with his sister, Susan. He heard her climb the stairs and go to her bedroom. It wasn't fair – she had been allowed to watch TV.

He must have fallen asleep because the next thing he knew his mother was calling him. Time to get up. It was eight o'clock. He had to eat his breakfast quickly and rush to school. His mum kept telling him to walk more quickly. He arrived just in time as the school bell rang. It was nine o'clock.

- Now write a sentence from the story.
  Remember to put a capital letter at the beginning and a full stop at the end!

____

____

Dear Helper,

Objective: to recognise full stops when reading.

First, read the story to your child. Then, read it again with your child, pausing at the full stops. Ask your child to put a ring around all the full stops. To reinforce work done at school, ask your child why the full stops are there (to show it is the end of a sentence). Now, help your child to write a sentence from the story, making sure that they remember to use a capital letter to begin and a full stop to finish the sentence.

Name:

Fruity full stops

- Read the sentences. What's missing?
- Write each sentence on the line.
  Don't forget to put in the full stops!

Apples can be red and green

Bananas are good for you

Oranges are nice and juicy

Pineapples are prickly

Lemons taste bitter

PHOTOCOPIABLE

Dear Helper,

Objective: to use full stops to mark sentences.

Read the sentences with your child and help them to rewrite them, making sure to put in a full stop at the end of each sentence. To reinforce work done at school, ask your child why the full stops are there (to show it is the end of a sentence).

Name:

Favourite fruit

- Look at the pictures and read the words.

tangerine

pineapple

orange

banana

lemon

pear

- Now answer the questions.

Do you like tangerines, pineapples, bananas, oranges, pears and lemons?

I like ______________________________________

____

____

Which is your favourite fruit?

____

____

Dear Helper,

Objective: to read unfamiliar words by using pictures.

Look at the pictures of fruit with your child and read the words underneath. Help your child answer the questions by writing a full sentence. They should list all the fruit they like and then choose their favourite.

Name:

The Little Red Hen: a picture story

- Look at the pictures and tell the story.

Who will help me plant this wheat?
Not I.
Who will help me cut this wheat?
Not I.
Who will help me grind this wheat?
Not I.
Who will help me bake this bread?
Not I.
Who will help me eat this bread?
I will.

Dear Helper,

Objective: to re-tell a known story from pictures.

Look carefully with your child at the pictures showing the story of *The Little Red Hen*. Read the speech bubbles together. Now, ask your child to re-tell the story, using the pictures as an aid. You could also try cutting up the pictures and seeing if your child can put them back in the correct order.

Name:

Slinky Malinki

- Read the story with your helper.
- Cut out the words and find them in the story.

Slinky Malinki
was blacker than black,
a stalking and lurking
adventurous cat.
He had bright yellow eyes,
a warbling wail
And a kink at the end
of his very long tail.
He was cheeky and cheerful,
friendly and fun,
he'd chase after leaves
and he'd roll in the sun.
But at night he was wicked
And fiendish and sly.
Through moonlight and shadow
He'd prowl and he'd pry.
He crept over fences,
He leaped over walls,
He poked into corners
And sneaked into halls.
What was he up to?
At night, to be brief,
Slinky Malinki
Turned into a
THIEF.

cat
eyes
sun
night
fences
walls
leaves
corners
tail
hall
thief
shadow

Dear Helper,

Objective: to match spoken to printed words.

Read the extract from the story *Slinky Malinki* by Lynley Dodd to your child. Talk about who Slinky Malinki is and what he's like. Now cut out the words above and spread them out. Read them to your child. Now re-read the extract, pointing to the words as you do so, and look for one word that you have cut out at a time. You might turn the words over when you have found them, or put them in a pile. You could also make up more sentences using these words.

PHOTOCOPIABLE

Name:

Tog the Dog

- Read this story.
- Find the rhyming words.

Have you heard of Tog the dog?

One day Tog went out for a jog.

He got lost in a fog,

tripped over a cog,

fell into a bog,

and frightened a frog.

Dear Helper,

Objective: to read a story independently and to look for rhyming words.

Read the story above with your child and talk about what happens. Now ask your child to try and read it alone. Now read it again and ask your child to supply the rhyming words while you pause. You could also highlight all the rhyming words and discuss the shared letter patterns.

Name:

T

Peace at Last

- Read the story with your helper.
- Put the pictures in the right order by numbering them 1–6.

Mr. Bear could not sleep. He tried sleeping in Baby Bear's room, but Baby Bear was pretending to be an aeroplane. Then Mr. Bear went downstairs. He tried the chair in the living room, then the kitchen. That did not work work so he went outside and even tried the car! Finally, he came back to his bed just as it was time to get up.

Dear Helper,

Objective: to sequence a story correctly.

Read the story with your child and then look carefully at the pictures. Now help your child to put them in the right order, either by cutting them out and sticking them on another piece of paper, or by numbering them 1– 6.

Name:

Describe the place

- Look at the pictures.
- Read the words. Draw arrows to show which words match which picture.

This is a very hot sunny place. There are a few straw huts which people live in. Children play with their animals. It is so hot they do not need to wear many clothes.

This is a very cold place. Snow and ice covers everywhere. People live in igloos and fish through holes in the ice. Polar bears live here too.

PHOTOCOPIABLE

Dear Helper,

Objective: to describe different settings.

Look carefully at the pictures above and then read the descriptions with your child. Now ask your child to say which words fit each picture. Help them to draw an arrow from the correct words to the matching picture.

Name:

Have you seen the crocodile?

- Look at the pictures.
- Fill in the missing words.

Have you seen the crocodile? "No" said the bee.

Have you seen the ________________? "No" said the ________________.

Have you seen the ________________? "No" said the ________________.

Have you seen the ________________? "No" said the ________________.

Dear Helper,

Objective: to substitute words in a patterned story.

Help your child to fill in the missing words by looking at the pictures.

T

Name:

Time for...?

- Read the poem with your helper.
- Draw a line between the words that rhyme.

Christopher Sweet tucked his feet
Down to the bottom
Of the warm, warm sheet.
How many times did the church clock strike?
One, two, three, four, five,
Six, seven, EIGHT!

Caroline Tate is always late
She's only just running
Through the old school gate!
How many times
Did the school bell chime?
One, two, three, four, five,
Six, seven, eight, NINE!

Oliver Lee can't wait for tea,
school's nearly finished for him and me!
How many rings till we're all free?
One, two THREE!

Nicola Head won't go to bed.
'Chase her up the stairs then'
her mother said.
How many times
Did the clock strike then?
One, two, three, four, five,
Six, seven, eight, nine, TEN!

Marilyn Heap is fast asleep;
Listen at the door
But you won't hear a peep!
How many times
Did the church clock strike?
One, two, three, four, five,
Six, seven, eight, nine, ten,
Eleven, twelve ... MIDNIGHT!

Judith Nicholls

Dear Helper,

Objective: to be able to predict rhyming words.

Read the poem to your child, then read it again but pause before saying the rhyming words, such as 'feet' and 'sheet'. Do this several times. You could try covering the rhyming words with your finger and asking your child to say what they are.

Name:

Can you help?

- Look at the pictures and finish the sentences.

I help my friend ______________________________

____

____

I help my teacher ____________________________

____

____

I help my mum ________________________________

____

____

I help my dad ________________________________

____

____

Dear Helper,

Objective: to write sentences to fit pictures.

Look carefully at each picture with your child. Talk about what is happening and help them to write a sentence to fit.

Name:

Our school day

- Look at the pictures and read the captions.

The whistle is blown at 9 o'clock
We line up on the playground.

The teacher calls the register.

We have assembly at 10 o'clock.

We have our dinner at 12 o'clock.

We have playtime at 2 o'clock.

Time to go home at 3 o'clock.

- Answer these questions.

What time is assembly? ______________________

How do you know when to line up? ______________________

____

What happens at 2 o'clock? ______________________

____

Dear Helper,

Objective: to read captions to pictures and answer questions.

Look carefully at the pictures above and read the captions with your child. Help them to answer the questions. Discuss with your child how their school day is different to that described.

Name:

T

How to make a jungle scene

- Read the instructions below and make the jungle scene.

You will need:
- Background picture
- Animal pictures
- Crayons
- Scissors
- Glue

1 Colour the background of the jungle.
2 Colour the animals carefully.
3 Cut out the animals.
4 Stick the animals carefully on the picture.
5 Admire your picture!

Dear Helper,

Objective: to read and follow simple instructions.

Read these instructions with your child. Make sure you have the necessary equipment and then help your child to read and follow each instruction carefully. Take the finished picture to school to show the teacher.

PHOTOCOPIABLE

Name:

Money for Monday

- Write a list of all the things you need to remember for different days of the week in school, such as dinner money on Mondays, recorder on Tuesdays, P.E. kit on Wednesdays, library books on Thursdays, spelling homework on Fridays.

Monday 	
Tuesday 	
Wednesday 	
Thursday 	
Friday 	

Dear Helper,

Objective: to write a list.

Talk to your child about things that they need to remember to take to school each day. Now encourage them to write a list, praising them for sensible attempts at writing words. Don't worry if every word is not spelled correctly. The aim is for your child to try and write independently.

Name:

W

Rhyming pairs

cliff	frill	fluff	click
spell	sniff	smell	bring
puff	floss	drill	sprung
cross	speck	trick	mess
dress	spring	fleck	clung

- Cut out the word cards above.
- Jumble them up and lay them face down.
- Take turns to turn a pair over. If you turn over a pair that rhymes, keep it. The one with the most pairs at the end wins.

Dear Helper,

Objective: to pick out rhyming words and to investigate their spellings.
Help your child to investigate the spellings of the words, pointing out the word endings *-ff*, *-ll*, *-ss*, *-ck* and *-ng*.

Name:

Make a word

sk	fl	gr	pl
sp	tw	br	dr
op	in	an	ip

- Play this game with your helper.
  - Cut out the cards. Some are word beginnings. Some are word endings.
  - Place all the cards face down on a table, then take turns to turn over two cards.
  - If you can make a word, for example: | fl | an | write the word on another piece of paper.
- The first person to collect 10 words wins.

Dear Helper,

Objective: to make words from word beginnings and word endings.

Play the game with your child. Encourage your child to say the word out loud. Help with writing if necessary. After the game, you could ask your child to choose a word ending card and write words that rhyme with the card, eg using *in – pin, chin, bin, spin*.

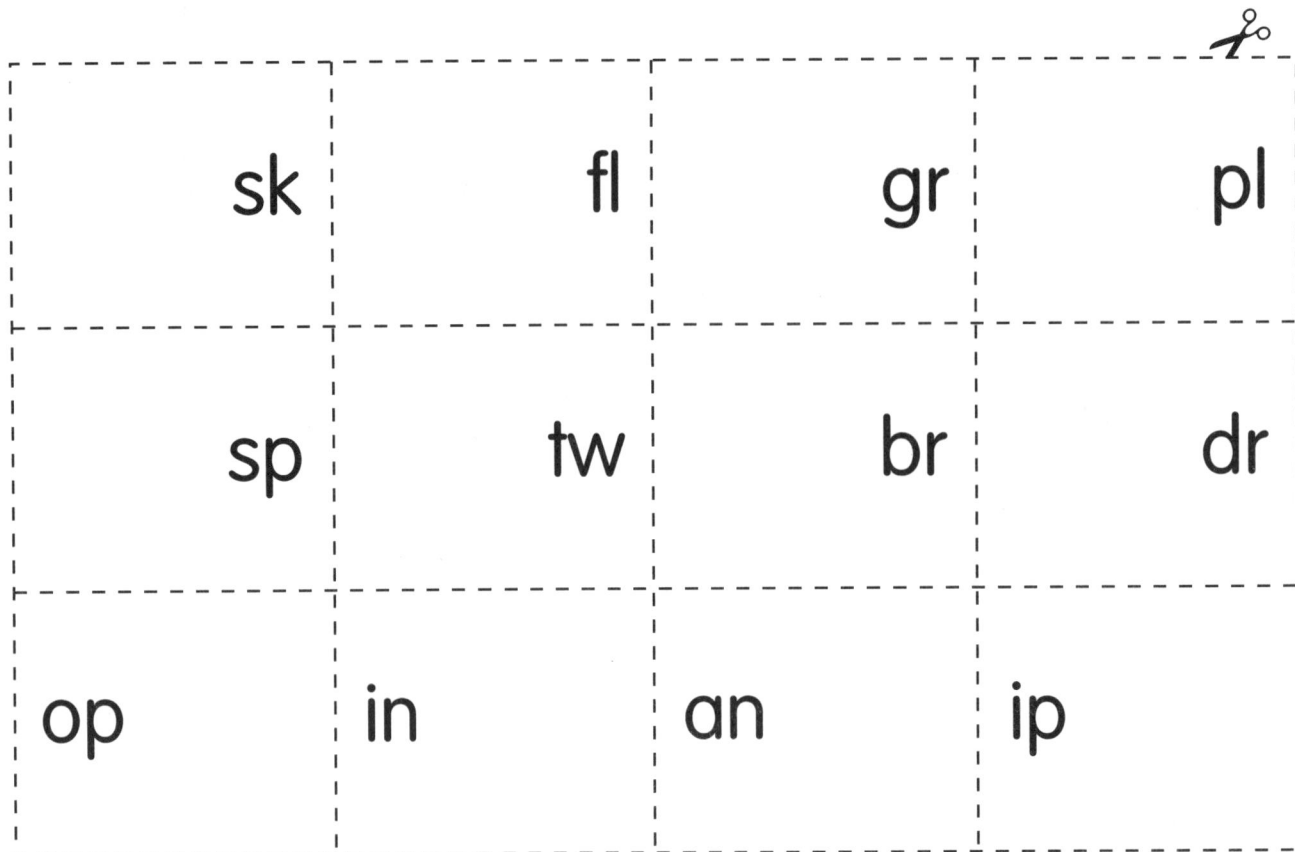

Name:

Roll a word

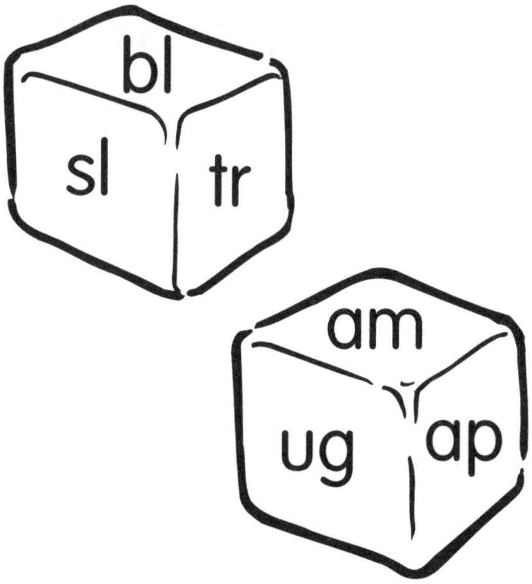

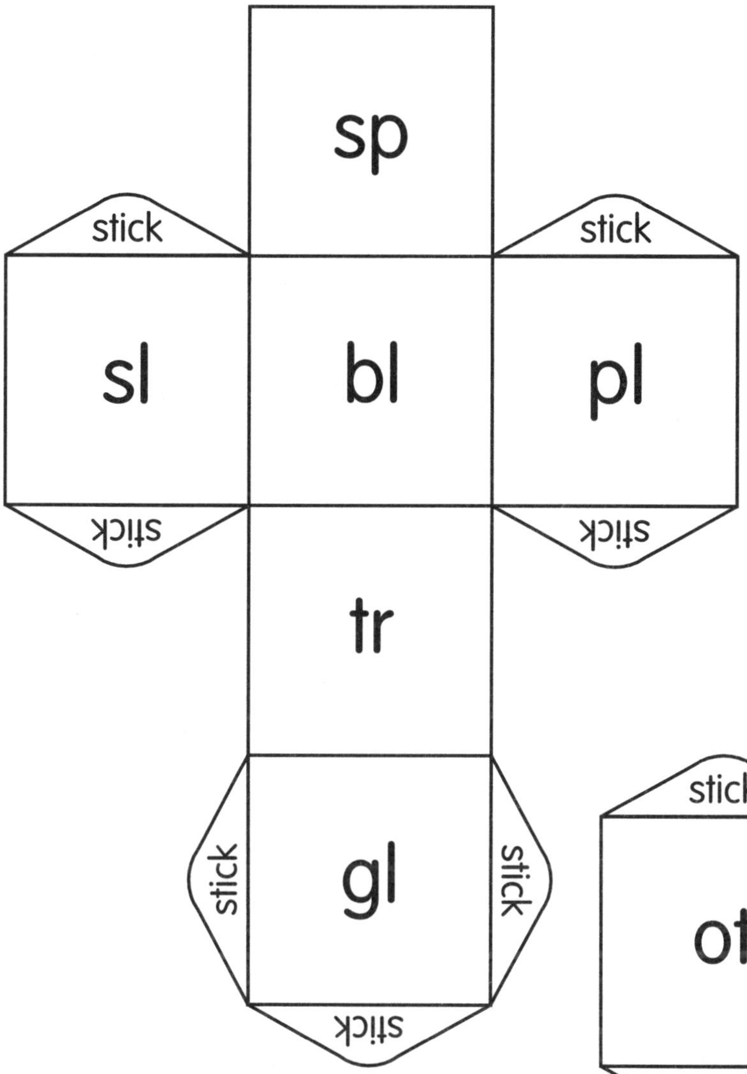

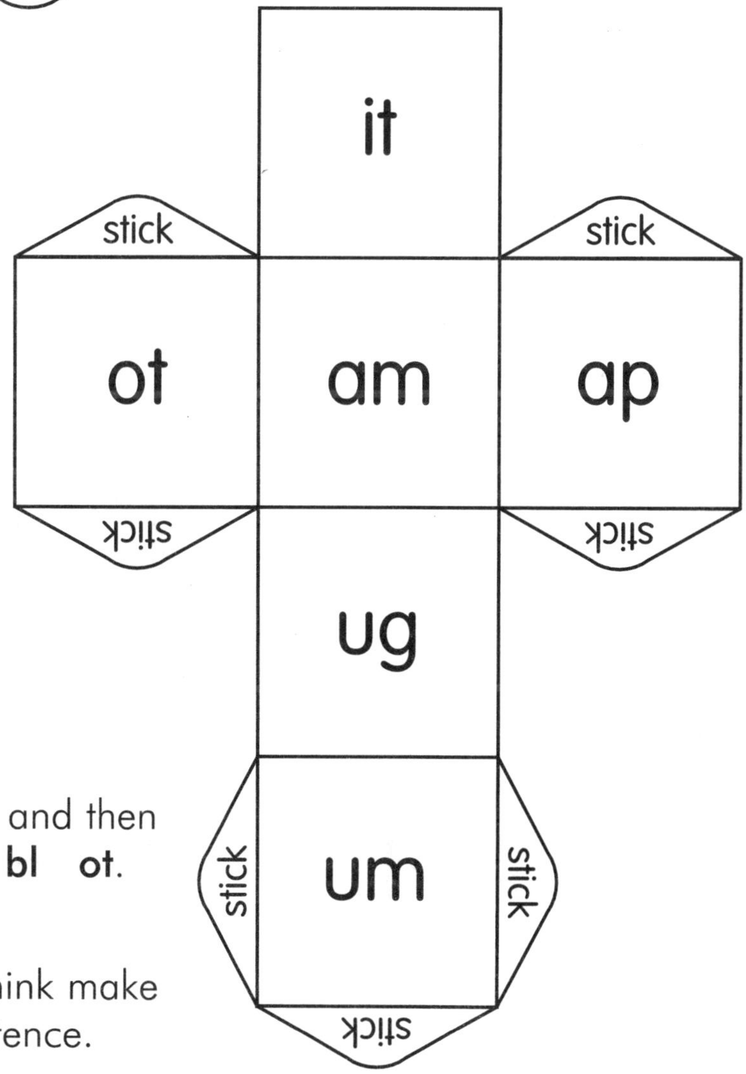

- Cut out the dice and fold and stick them to make cubes.
- Roll the dice to make words. Sound out the word beginning and then the word ending, for example: **bl ot**. Does it make sense?
- Make a list of the words you think make sense and put them into a sentence.

Dear Helper,

Objective: to make words from word beginnings and word endings.

Help your child make the dice. Roll the dice with them. Encourage them to say the word out loud. Talk about whether or not the word makes sense. If it does, help your child to use it in a sentence.

W

Name:

Letter sounds

- Say each letter sound you hear in the following words.
- Use a pencil to draw a line between the sounds.

p / l / a / n / k

blink	blast	plump
drift	flint	drink
flask	grand	slept
spend	frost	twist

PHOTOCOPIABLE

Dear Helper,

Objective: to help identify letter sounds in words for spelling.

Help your child to make the sound of each letter in order to blend them together to make the sound of the whole word. Drawing a pencil line between each sound will help your child to distinguish the individual letter sounds for spelling.

Name:

Pick a pair

sand	help	mist	last
gulp	band	cast	pulp
mind	blast	fist	kind
spend	yelp	mend	rind
twist	past	find	list

- Cut out the word cards above.
- Jumble them up and lay them face down.
- Take turns to turn a pair over. If you turn over a pair that rhymes, keep it. The one with the most pairs at the end wins.

Dear Helper,

Objective: to pick out rhyming words and to investigate their spellings.

Help your child to investigate the spellings of the words, pointing out the word endings *-nd*, *-lp* and *-st*.

PHOTOCOPIABLE

Name:

Slide a word

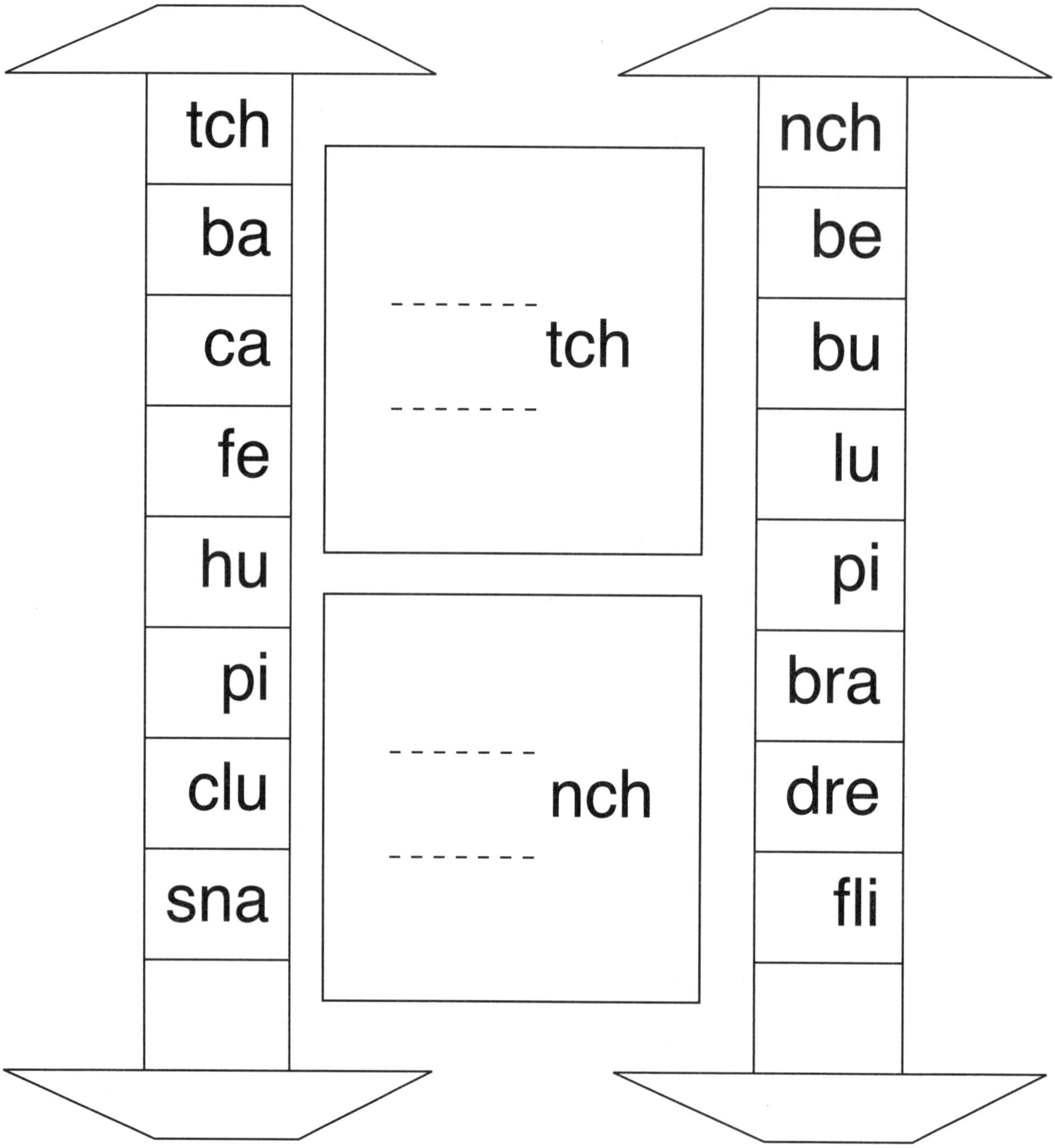

- Cut out the word slide pieces. If possible, stick them onto card so they last longer.
- Cut along the slits in the word ending cards and thread the long strips through from the back of the card.
- Read the words you find as you slide the strip along.

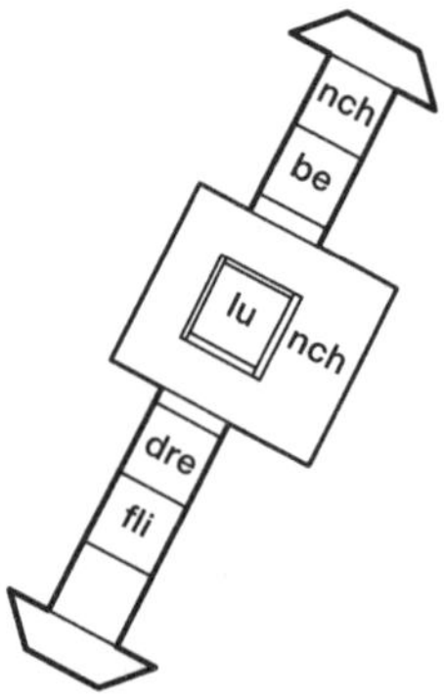

Dear Helper,

Objective: to make, read and say words using word endings -*tch* and -*nch*.
Help your child to make the word slides. Then, encourage your child to read and say the words they make using the word slides.

Name:

Guess the game

- Read the story aloud and fill in the spaces with **s** or **ss**.
- Can you guess the game Jennifer played? ____

Hint: It ends with ss!

Jennifer joined her cla____ just before playtime.

'How wa____ the tournament?' asked Mi____ Richards, her teacher.

'The game lasted over an hour. It wa ____ very difficult and I had to gue____ a lot of the move____. At times I got cro____ with myself for rushing. Then I managed to place my Queen next to the King, which wa____ a great move!'

'Wa____ Mr Harding there, Jennifer?'

'Ye____. He made me feel le____ nervous and he made a fu____ of me after the game. Mum and Dad blew me a ki____.'

'Well, Jennifer, we are all waiting to know if you won.'

'Ye____! It was checkmate!'

Dear Helper,

Objective: to investigate and spell words ending in -s and -ss.

Read the text with your child and help to predict the missing words. Discuss the spelling of the words and decide on one -s or two -ss.

PHOTOCOPIABLE

Name:

Sort the rhymes

- Sort these rhyming words by the spelling of their rhyming endings.
- Place them correctly in the grid below.

bear	care	pear	bare	tear
snare	glare	hare	share	fare
stare	rare	flare	mare	swear

ear	are	other words

Dear Helper,

Objective: to recognise and sort common spelling patterns within words.

Point out the different spelling patterns that make the same sound. Discuss with your child other words that rhyme and find out how they are spelled.

Name:

Spell well (3)

Remember!
Look at the word carefully.
Say the word aloud,
then **cover** the word while
you try to **write** the word.
Now **check** to see if it is right.

Look and Say	Cover	Write	Check
so			
but			
next			
because			
then			
after			
when			

Dear Helper,

Objective: to learn to spell common words.

Help your child to spell these words by looking carefully at the letters, and saying the word aloud. Then, fold the paper so the word is covered. Encourage them to try and write the word. They should check their writing against the printed word. Lastly, make up sentences using the word.

Name:

Pick a position

- Fill in the missing words under the pictures.
  Choose one of these words:

under in down up over out

Jack __ __ a box

Jack __ __ __ of his box

Climbing __ __ the slide

Sliding __ __ __ __ the slide

Going __ __ __ __ a bridge

Going __ __ __ __ __ a bridge

Dear Helper,

Objective: to spell words that occur frequently and to expect reading to make sense.

Help your child to predict the words that are missing and choose appropriately from the list. Point out that each line represents a letter.

Name:

W

Sh, sh, sh!

- Add **sh** to the spaces.
- Then read and say the word.

____e	____ow	____ake
____ed	____ape	____ut
____ell	____ore	____ine
swi____	wa____	cra____
pu____	fre____	____ould
sun____ine	wi____	sea____ore

- Now write some sentences using some of the words.

____

____

____

____

Dear Helper,

Objective: to read and spell words that contain the *sh* sound and to use them in a sentence.
Help your child to complete the spellings of the words above. They should then read each one aloud to you. Choose some of the words with your child and use them to make sentences.

Name:

A place poem

- Choose a place you know well, such as your bedroom, your classroom, the kitchen, or a shop.
  Write a poem about the place using some of these words:

outside inside down up under over
round through beside behind

Here is an example:

Outside my bedroom it is dark
Inside I am snug in bed
With my teddy beside me

- Give your poem a title.

PHOTOCOPIABLE

Dear Helper,

Objective: to read the words and use them in a meaningful way to write a short poem.
Help your child choose a familiar place and some of the position words to write a descriptive poem.

Name:

Likes and dislikes

What do you like? What do you dislike?

- Complete the following sentences to write about your likes and dislikes.

I like going to bed because

I dislike going to bed because

I like getting up in the morning because

I dislike getting up in the morning because

I like lunchtimes at school because

I dislike lunchtimes at school because

I like going on holiday because

I dislike going on holiday because

Dear Helper,

Objective: to write in sentences and use full stops appropriately.

Help your child by talking to them first about their likes and dislikes. Then help them to compose a short sentence, making sure they always finish with a full stop.

Name:

The Clever Cockerel and the Crafty Fox

The following sentences tell the story of a clever cockerel and a crafty fox, but someone has forgotten to include the capital letters and the full stops.

- Put capital letters and full stops where you think they should go.

one day a crafty fox had a plan to catch a clever cockerel

the fox was always thinking of plans to catch the cockerel but he hadn't managed it yet

the crafty fox went to the barn where the cockerel lived

the crafty fox tricked the cockerel and threw a sack over the cockerel's head

the fox ran off as fast as he could with the sack over his shoulder

the clever cockerel took a pair of scissors out of his waistcoat pocket and cut a hole big enough for him to get through

quick as a wink the cockerel put a stone as heavy as himself into the sack and ran as fast as he could back to his barn

soon the fox arrived at his den and emptied out the sack over a pot of boiling water

the stone crashed into the pot and the boiling water splashed all over the silly fox

the clever cockerel laughed when he heard the silly fox yell

- Now read the story with your helper.

PHOTOCOPIABLE

Dear Helper,

Objective: to use capital letters and full stops correctly.

Help your child to read the sentences and discuss where to put capital letters and full stops. Then, read the whole story through together.

Name:

How would you feel?

How would you feel in these situations?

- Look at each picture and write a sentence under each one to describe your feelings.

Dear Helper,

Objective: to write in sentences using capital letters and full stops correctly.

Discuss each picture with your child, asking them how they would feel in the same situation, and perhaps offering an idea of how you would feel. Then, help them to compose a sentence or two for each picture that describes their feelings.

Name:

Two Little Bears

- The capital letters are missing from the beginning of sentences in the following story. Put them in the correct place.

mother Bear and her two cubs Ben and Bella lived in a forest in North America. the two cubs liked to play hide and seek. one day Ben hid where he thought no one would find him. his sister looked everywhere but could not find him so she began to cry. along came mother bear sniffing for Ben. she lifted her head and sniffed the air. then she smiled as she saw Ben hiding in the branches of a tree. suddenly Ben lost his grip and crashed to the ground. bella laughed and growled a friendly growl. she was very glad her mother had found him.

Dear Helper,

Objective: to use capital letters for the start of sentences.

Read the story with your child and help put the capital letters in the right place. Talk about how a capital letter always follows a full stop.

Name:

T

Rhyming story

Play hide and seek once then play it again.	We go in to the house and up the stairs.
We go through the gate and down the lane.	I have a dragon who plays with me.
To make tea for tigger and my teddy bears.	Everywhere I go she comes with me.

The pictures are in the correct order but the rhyming sentences are jumbled.

- Cut out the words and pictures.
- Match the words to the pictures to make a rhyming story.
- Paste them onto a separate sheet.

Dear Helper,

Objective: to read the captions and match them to the pictures.

Help your child to read the captions and use the rhyming endings as a guide to matching them to the correct pictures.

PHOTOCOPIABLE

Name:

Little Samantha's day

Little Samantha shouts 'It's all gone!'

Little Samantha asleep with her bear.

Little Samantha puts jam on her bread.

Little Samantha eats sausages at one.

Little Samantha jumps out of her bed.

Little Samantha reads books in a chair.

- Put these sentences in the correct order to find out about little Samantha's day.
- First cut out the boxes.
- Then paste the sentences and pictures onto a separate sheet in the right order.

Hint: Put pairs of lines together that rhyme!

Dear Helper,

Objective: to use rhyme and sense to re-order sentences into a sequenced and meaningful poem.
Discuss the pictures and descriptions with your child and use the rhyme endings to help order the sentences correctly.

Name:

Chocolate charmer

- Some important words are missing from the recipe below. Choose the correct words from the list below and write them in the spaces under the pictures so the recipe makes sense. The first one has been done for you.

break slice top scoop decorate
chill stir mix eat

stir		

- Now, you might like to try making it with the help of an adult!

Dear Helper,

Objective: to read unfamiliar words and to make sense of what they mean.

Many of the words above will be unfamiliar to your child. To help your child understand the meaning of the words talk about the action that is occurring in the picture.

Name:

Book covers

- Look at these book covers. What do you think the stories will be about? Talk about them with your helper.

Dear Helper,

Objective: to predict what a story will be about from the book cover and to discuss preferences and give reasons.

Discuss with your child what is being portrayed on the book covers and ask which books they would prefer to read and why. Share your own ideas and preferences as well.

Name:

The Three Billy Goats Gruff

- Ask your helper to read this story with you.

Once upon a time there were three goats: Little Billy Goat Gruff, Big Billy Goat Gruff and Great Big Billy Goat Gruff. They lived in a field, but the goats wanted to eat the grass in another field at the other side of the river. To get to the field they had to cross the bridge, but under the bridge lived a nasty, horrible, goat-eating Troll.

One day Little Billy Goat Gruff felt brave and decided to cross the bridge. So off he trotted, trip-trap, trip-trap over the bridge.

'Who is going trip-trap, trip-trap over my bridge?' roared the Troll.

'Little Billy Goat Gruff,' replied the goat.

'Then I will eat you up!' snarled the Troll.

'No! No! Do not eat me! I am too little. Eat Big Billy Goat Gruff when he comes over the bridge. He is much fatter.'

'Mmmm, yes, I'd rather have a fatter goat,' answered the Troll.

So Little Billy Goat Gruff ran trip-trap, trip-trap over the bridge.

Then Big Billy Goat Gruff went trip-trap, trip-trap over the bridge. The same thing happened.

'Mmmm, yes, I'd rather have a fatter goat,' said the Troll.

So Big Billy Goat Gruff ran trip-trap, trip-trap over the bridge.

At last Great Big Billy Goat Gruff decided to cross the bridge and so off he went, trip-trap, trip-trap over the bridge. Exactly the same thing happened.

'Who is going trip-trap, trip-trap over my bridge?' roared the Troll.

'Great Big Billy Goat Gruff,' replied the goat.

'Then I will eat you up!' snarled the Troll, and he jumped onto the bridge.

Great Big Billy Goat Gruff pointed his horns and charged at the Troll. His sharp horns caught the Troll and tossed him into the air, over the bridge and into the deep river.

'Ow! Ow! Ow!' cried the Troll.

'Hee! Hee ! Hee!' laughed the goats, and all three ate the grass on the other side of the river.

- Now, tell the story to your helper or someone else.

Dear Helper,

Objective: to re-tell a story giving the main points in sequence.

Read the story of 'The Three Billy Goats Gruff' with or to your child. Then, ask your child to re-tell the story back to you, helping them as necessary with prompts to remember the sequence of events.

Name:

What they might say

- Draw a line to match the speech bubbles to the pictures.

No! No! No! Don't eat me. I'm too little.

Who's going trip-trap, trip-trap over my bridge?

Ow! Ow! Ow! Ow!

We'd like to eat the grass on the other side of the river.

Dear Helper,

Objective: to sequence the story of 'The Three Billy Goats Gruff' by matching the speech bubbles to the appropriate picture.

Help your child to match the speech bubbles to the pictures and encourage your child to read what is said with appropriate expression.

Name:

T

Beginnings and endings

- Read what it says inside each book and decide whether it is a beginning or an ending to a story. Write either beginning or ending appropriately in the space beneath.

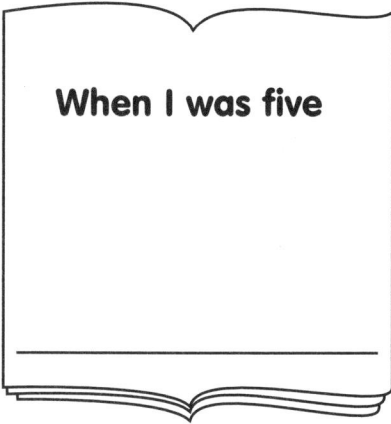

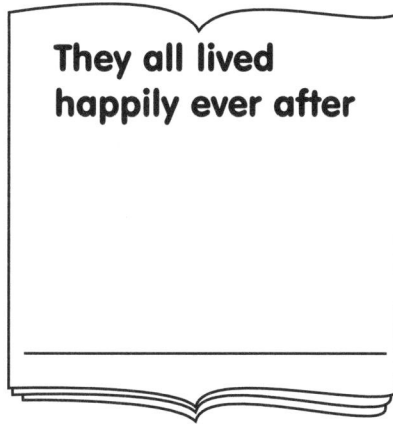

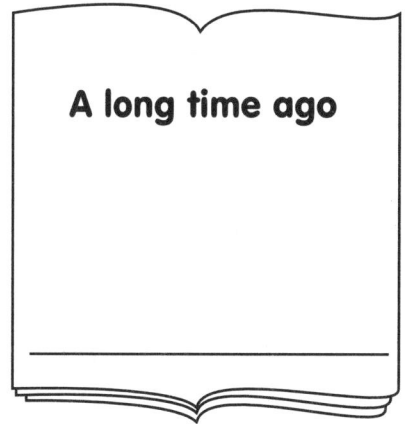

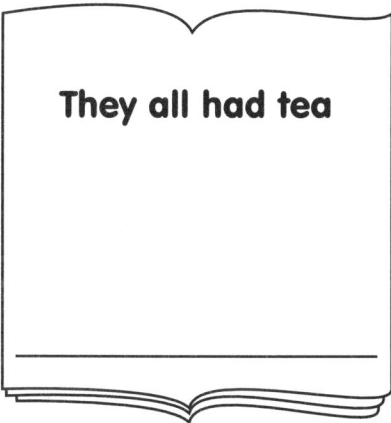

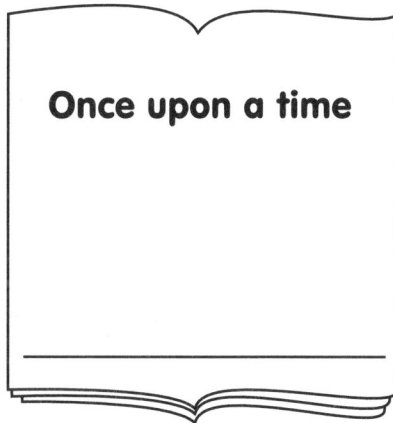

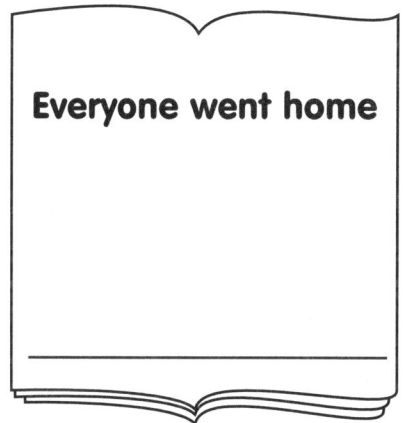

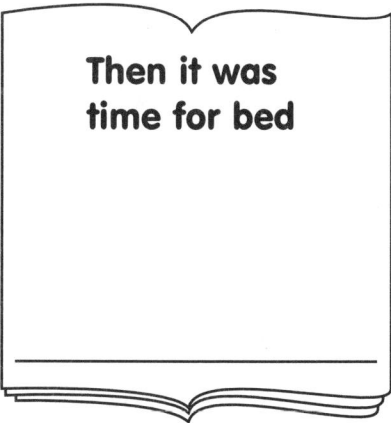

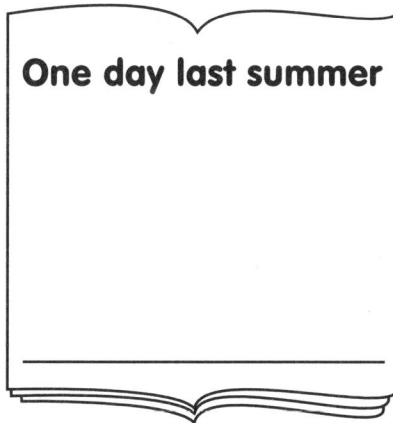

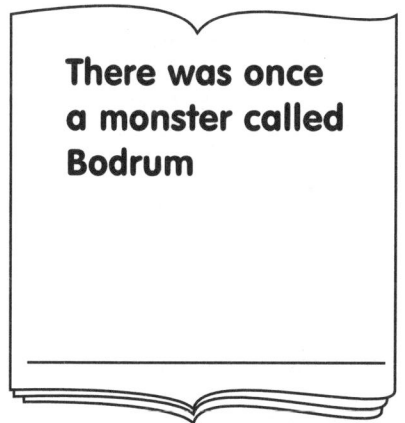

When I was five

______

They all lived happily ever after

______

A long time ago

______

They all had tea

______

Once upon a time

______

Everyone went home

______

Then it was time for bed

______

One day last summer

______

There was once a monster called Bodrum

______

Dear Helper,

Objective: to be able to identify beginnings and endings of stories.

Help your child to read what is in the boxes. Discuss whether they could be the beginning or an ending and relate them to stories they may have read.

T

Name:

Be a poet

- Choose a subject, such as your favourite toy, sweet, food, game or pet.
- Write a poem, using one word each to describe:
  - its colour
  - the sound it makes
  - how it feels
  - what it smells like
  - what it tastes like
  - what it is

  Use the back of this sheet or another piece of paper.

Your finished poem might look like this:

colour........................ Yellow

sound........................ Crunch

feel............................ Crinkly

smell.......................... Lemony

taste........................... Sharp

name.......................... Sherbert lemon

Dear Helper,

Objective: to write a poem using a model.

First, help your child choose a favourite item. Then talk about it with your child, perhaps jotting down some of the words used. Select the best words to fit each aspect of the poem and help your child to write these in the poem format. Read the poem with your child. Ask: *Does it read the way you want it to, or is there anything we need to change?*

Name:

T

Create-a-story game

name	name
met	met
on	on
they went to	they went to
on the way they met	on the way they met
who said	who said
so they all	so they all

- Your helper will explain how to play this game with another person. You will create some funny stories.

Dear Helper,

Objective: to create a funny story.

Cut out the story strips and give one to each player. Each player writes down the name of someone they know, then folds over the name so it can't be seen and passes the strip to the other player. Continue by passing the strips back and forth until the story strips are completed. Make more strips so others can play. Then, read the stories aloud (if you can without laughing!).

PHOTOCOPIABLE

Name:

What's the story?

- Look at the picture and talk with your helper about what you think is happening.
- Write a short story about it. Think about:
  - Which bit of the picture are you going to use to start your story?
  - Will it have a happy ending?

PHOTOCOPIABLE

Dear Helper,

Objective: to use the picture to write a simple story.

Talk about what is happening in the picture. Discuss where the story might start and how it is going to end. Then, help your child to write a short story based on the events in the picture. If necessary, write for your child, reading the story together as you go along.

Name:

Fiction or non-fiction?

- Look at the book covers.
- Write underneath each one which you think it is – fiction or non-fiction. Could some be both?

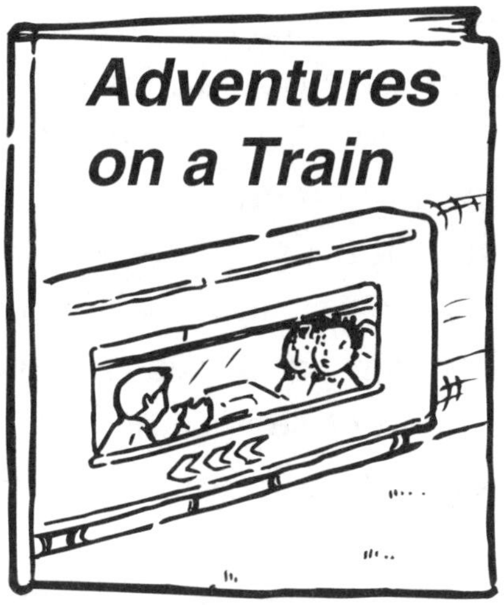

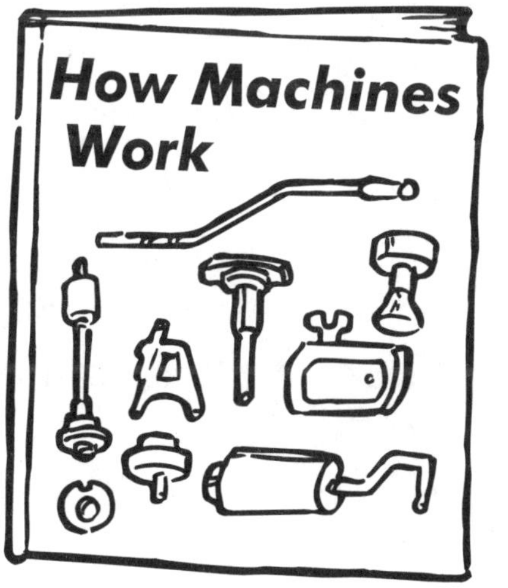

Dear Helper,

Objective: to understand and use the terms 'fiction' and 'non-fiction' and to predict what a book might be about from its cover.

Make sure your child understands that *fiction* is made up, whereas *non-fiction* is fact. Help your child to talk about and explain the decisions they make about whether the books are fiction or non-fiction.

PHOTOCOPIABLE

T Name:

All about seeds

- Read 'All about seeds' with your helper.

All about seeds

Most plants make seeds in order to make new plants. The plant forms seeds when its flowers stop blooming. Sometimes you can see the old flower at the end of a pea pod or at the end of a rose hip. In a pea pod the seeds are in a row inside the pod and we like eating them. In a rose hip the seeds are very tiny. We don't eat those seeds, but we can eat the covering called the hip when it is made into rose hip syrup. We eat lots of seeds such as lentils, beans, peanuts, and pumpkin and sunflower seeds that we can roast and scatter on bread. The coconut is one of the biggest seeds that grow. We also like to eat the fruit and vegetable coverings that protect seeds, such as melon, pumpkin, apple, peach, orange, cucumber, tomato, cherries, and lots more.

- Now answer these questions. Write in sentences.

  The answers have been started for you.

Question 1. Why do plants make seeds?

Answer Plants make seeds ______________________________.

Question 2. When do the seeds start to form?

Answer Seeds start to form when ______________________________.

Question 3. How are the peas arranged in the pod?

Answer Peas are arranged in ______________________________.

Question 4. Which is one of the biggest seeds that grow?

Answer The ______________ is one of the biggest seeds that grow.

Question 5. Which part of the cherry do you think will grow into a new plant?

Answer I think the ______________ will grow into a new plant.

Dear Helper,

Objective: to read and understand non-fiction.

Read or help your child to read the text. Talk about it. Ask: *Is it a story or is it factual? What is it telling us about?* Assist your child in completing the answers to the questions, supporting them by re-reading relevant bits of the text.

Name:

T

Indexes

These two non-fiction books need indexes.

- Sort the words and write them in alphabetical order to make an index for each book. List the words, putting their page number next to them.

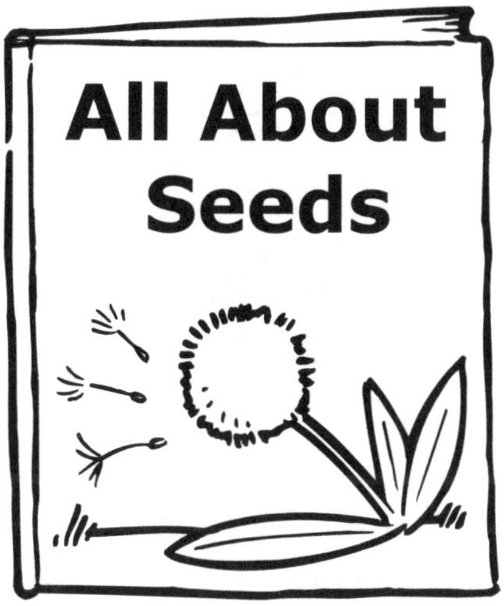

seeds	1
dandelion	5
conker	4
wind	5
keys	4
burrs	4
nuts	3
pips	2
stones	2
pods	2

Index

	page
burrs	4
conkers	4

eggs	2
caterpillar	2
butterfly	1
chrysalis	3
wings	4
nettles	2
flowers	5
nectar	5
leaves	2
legs	3

Index

	page
butterfly	1
caterpillar	2

Dear Helper,

Objective: to sort a jumbled list of words into alphabetical order for an index.

Help your child to read the words in the lists. Discuss how to order the words into alphabetical order, and ask questions such as which word would come first and why. If two words begin with the same letter, discuss the importance of the second letter in ordering the words. Look at some books at home that have indexes.

T

Name:

Order! Order!

- Sort the words into alphabetical order and write new lists. The first one has been done for you.

apple	ant	bee		fur		lime	
axe	apple	bat		foam		lace	
ant	axe	black		first		luck	

good		coat		dusk		here	
green		cane		dark		home	
gate		clap		drink		hive	

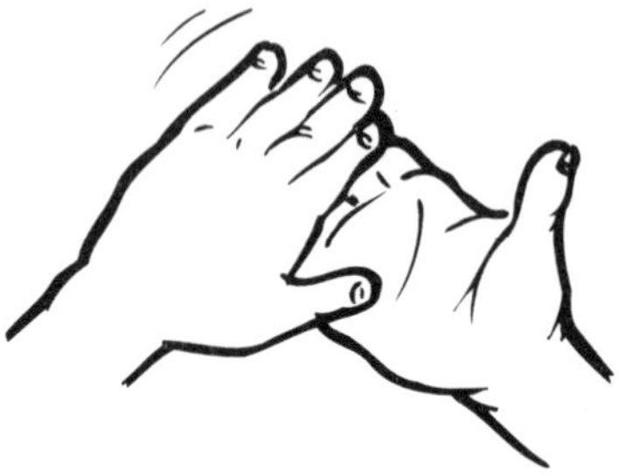

junk		man		name		oar	
jar		meet		net		open	
jet		moat		nine		one	

Dear Helper,

Objective: to practise putting words in alphabetical order.

Discuss with your child that when words begin with the same letter, it is the second letter in the words that help you to decide their alphabetical order. If your child needs extra support, it might help to write out the alphabet for reference.

Name:

T

Using dictionaries

- Arrange the following words in alphabetical order.
- Look up their meaning in a dictionary.
- Compose a sentence for each word.

first **laugh** **again** **water**

Write your sentences here:

1 ____________________

____

2 ____________________

____

3 ____________________

____

4 ____________________

____

Dear Helper,

Objective: to be able to use a simple dictionary and to understand its alphabetical organisation.
Discuss the way a dictionary is organised in alphabetical order. Help your child to find the words in the dictionary, read their meaning and write a simple sentence for each word to show they understand the meaning.

PHOTOCOPIABLE

Name:

Label the house

- The following words describe parts of a house.

door tiles window roof

gutter bricks chimney porch

- Use them to help you write labels for the picture.
- Draw a line from the part of the house to the label like the one that is already done for you.

Dear Helper,

Objective: to label a picture.

Help your child to read the words in order to label correctly the parts of the house.

PHOTOCOPIABLE

Name:

T

Making a fruit salad

The pictures below show how to make a fruit salad.

- Write a simple explanation underneath each picture.
  Say what is happening. Some words are given to help you.

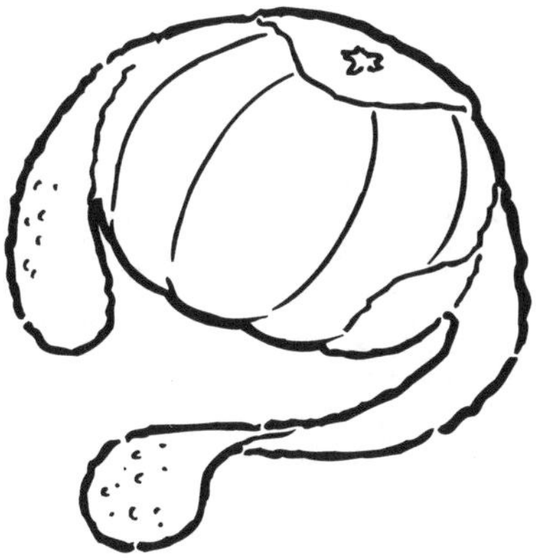

Cut ______________________

____

Peel ______________________

____

Slice ______________________

____

Squeeze ______________________

____

Dear Helper,

Objective: to write simple instructions.

Explain to your child that what is written should explain what is happening in the picture, for example: *Cut the apple*. They should end up with a recipe for making fruit salad in words as well as pictures.

T

Name:

Questions, questions

- Look at the picture.
- Write five questions you could ask someone about the picture.

Write your questions here:

1 __________

2 __________

3 __________

4 __________

5 __________

PHOTOCOPIABLE

Dear Helper,

Objective: to write simple questions.

Discuss the picture with your child and help to raise questions. Assist your child in writing some of the questions, for example: *What shop is next to the butchers? How many children are on scooters?*

Name:

Sort the sound

- Sort the words by the way the **oo** sound is spelled. Write them under the correct heading in the table below.
- Can you think of other words you could add to the table?

moon	fruit	boot	lute	root
chute	soon	suit	coot	brute
flute	scoot	shoot	spoon	noon
flew	clue	blue	chew	true
zoom	prune	food	mood	soon

oo	ui	u-e	ue	ew

Dear Helper,

Objective: to recognise different ways to spell the oo sound.

Help your child to read the words in the grid, giving particular attention to the spelling in order that they can be sorted and entered correctly on the table.

W Name:

Phoneme sounds (1)

- Say each sound you hear in the following words.
- Use a pencil to draw a line between the sounds.

s / p / oo / n

spoon	moon	root
oat	goat	boat
train	rain	drain
meet	street	fleet
tie	pie	lie

PHOTOCOPIABLE

Dear Helper,

Objective: to identify the separate sounds in words to make spelling them easier.

A phoneme is the smallest unit of sound in a word. Help your child to distinguish the vowel sound made up of two letters in the words above. Drawing a pencil line between each sound will help your child to distinguish the individual letter sounds and the single vowel sound made by the two vowel letters.

Name:

Word slide

ew
bl
dr
f
fl
n
str
st

_______ ew

_______ ue

ue
bl
c
cl
d
gl
h
tr

- Cut out the word slide pieces. If possible, stick them onto card so they last longer.
- Cut along the slits in the word ending cards and thread the long strips through from the back of the card.
- Read the words you find as you slide the strip along.

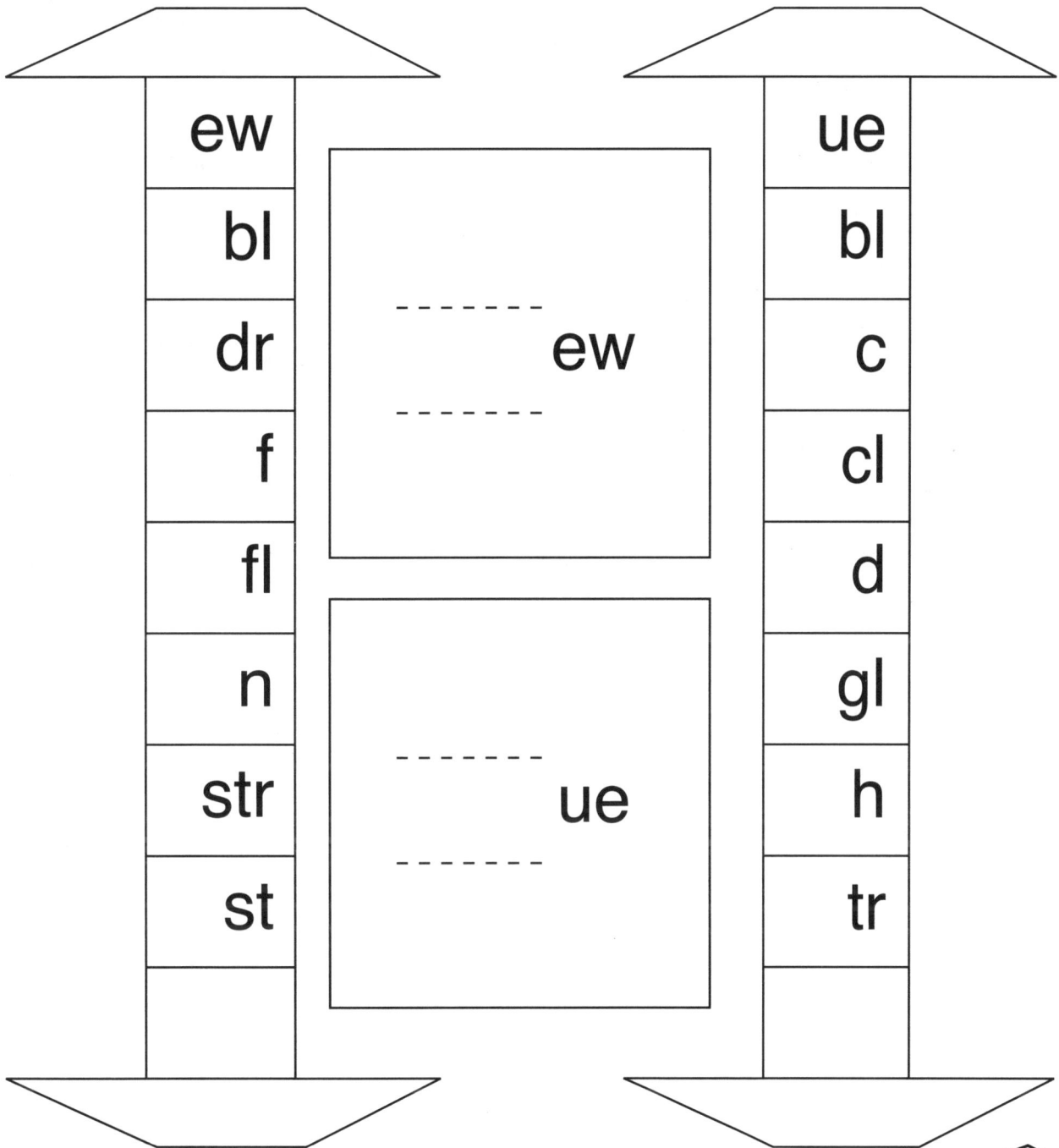

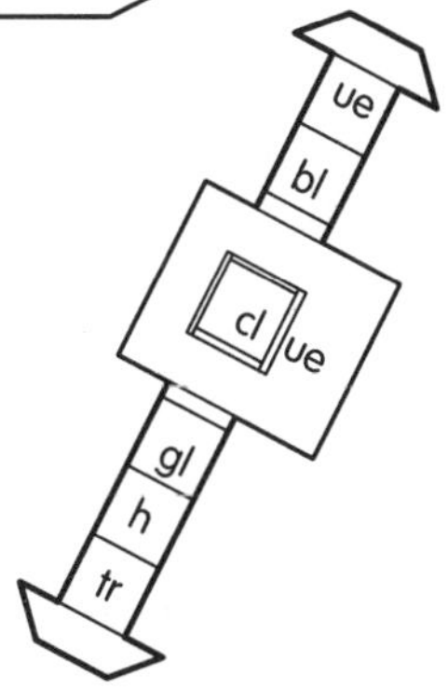

Dear Helper,

Objective: to make, read, say, and spell words using word endings -*ew* and -*ue*.
Help your child to read, say and spell the words, sounding out the words (eg *b/l/ue*) and pointing out the spellings of the oo sound.

W Name:

Long vowel sounds (1)

- Read aloud the words in the grid.
- Cover **y** words with a blue counter.
- Cover **igh** words with a red counter.
- Cover **ie** words with a green counter.

why	spy	sigh	by
cry	lie	try	nigh
high	my	dry	fry
pie	shy	tie	sly

- How many different spellings can you find for the sound **ie** as in **pie**?
- Use some of the words to make sentences. Write your sentences here:

1 ________________________________

2 ________________________________

3 ________________________________

4 ________________________________

5 ________________________________

Dear Helper,

Objective: to recognise some of the common spelling patterns for the long vowel sound *ie*. (The short vowel sound would be *i* as in 'pig' but the long vowel sound would be *i* as in 'pie').

Help your child to carry out the task and discuss the different spelling patterns *y*, *ie*, and *igh*. Use different coins or dried beans if you don't have counters. Then, encourage your child to use some of the words in sentences. If necessary, give help with writing the sentences.

Name:

Long vowel sounds (2)

- Read aloud the words in the grid.
- Cover **o** words with a blue counter.
- Cover **oe** words with a red counter.
- Cover **ow** words with a green counter.

toe	row	go	snow
no	woe	crow	bow
slow	grow	foe	throw
hoe	show	so	low

- How many different spellings can you find for the sound **ow** as in **low**?
- Use some of the words to make sentences. Write your sentences here:

1 ___

2 ___

3 ___

4 ___

5 ___

Dear Helper,

Objective: to recognise some of the common spelling patterns for the long vowel sound oe. (The short vowel sound would be o as in 'cot' but the long vowel sound would be oe as in 'toe').

Help your child to carry out the task and discuss the different spelling patterns o, oe, and ow. Use different coins or dried beans if you don't have counters. Then, encourage your child to use some of the words in sentences. If necessary, give help with writing the sentences.

PHOTOCOPIABLE

Name:

Pussy Cat, Pussy Cat

- Read the poem and listen for the long vowel sounds **ee** (as in **been**) and **ai** (as in **train**).
- Make two collections, one of the words you find with the sound **ee** in them, and another for words with the sound **ai** in them.
- Sort them by their different spellings and put them in the grids.

'Pussy Cat, Pussy Cat, where have you been?'

'I've been on a train to see the Queen.'

'Pussy Cat, Pussy Cat, what did she say?'

'Pleased to meet you, but you can't stay all day.'

'Pussy Cat, Pussy Cat, did you think she was mean?'

'Oh no! She was busy, after all she's the Queen.'

ee	e	ea

ai	ay

PHOTOCOPIABLE

Dear Helper,

Objective: to identify the long vowel sounds by their sound and learn their different spelling patterns.
Help your child to read the poem. It is best to track one sound at a time, so, first of all, help your child to listen and pick out all the ee sounds, writing them in the grid. Then, do the same for the *ai* sounds. You may wish to continue this activity using other texts and adding to the number of spelling patterns in the grids.

Name:

W

Phoneme sounds (2)

- Say each sound you hear in the following words.
- Use a pencil to draw a line between the sounds.

b / l / ue **sh / a / ke**

week	plain	bloat
fly	true	flew
show	shoe	shake
cheese	bloom	tight
spoon	crown	bright

Dear Helper,

Objective: to identify the separate sounds in words to make spelling them easier.

A phoneme is the smallest unit of sound in a word. Help your child to distinguish the sounds in each word. Drawing a pencil line between each sound will help your child to distinguish the sounds.

Name:

Adding 'ing'

When you add **ing** to words, some words will stay as they are:

1. **kiss + ing = kissing**

but some words change:

2. **hope + ing = hoping**

- With your helper talk about and write what happened in example 2.

____

3. **shop + ing = shopping**

- With your helper talk about and write what happened in example 3.

____

- Add **ing** to the words in the grid and write the new words in the middle column.
- Which numbered example above does each of these follow? Write a number in the last column. The first one has been done for you.

go	going	1
foam	______	
kiss	______	
come	______	
care	______	
make	______	
skip	______	
hop	______	
run	______	

Dear Helper,

Objective: to investigate and learn spellings of verbs (action words) ending in -ing.

Using the script preceding the activity, help your child to explain what is happening to the original word when adding *-ing*. Write your child's explanation, or support them in their own writing. Then, support your child with the activity.

Name:

Animal sounds and actions

- Talk to your helper about words ending in **ing** that describe the sounds and actions these animals make.
- Write your words around the pictures, like the one that has been started for you.
- Check your spellings in a dictionary.

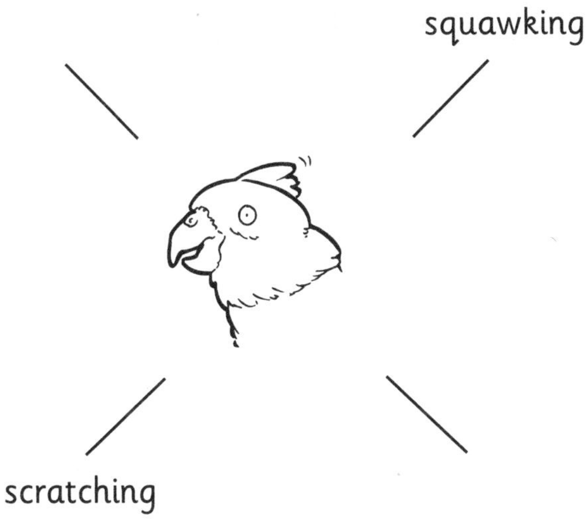

Dear Helper,

Objective: to investigate and learn spellings of verbs (action words) with *-ing* endings.

Support your child by talking about the animals, the sounds they make and their movements and actions. You could mime some of the actions and see if your child can guess them.

Name:

Adding 'ed' or 'd'

When you want to write about something that has happened in the past, some words need to change and we add **ed**. Some words will stay as they are:

kiss + **ed** = **kissed**

For words that already end in **e** we only need to add **d**:

hope + **d** = **hoped**

For other words ending in a single consonant, we add the same consonant and then **ed**:

shop + **p** + **ed** = **shopped**

- Change these words to the past tense.
  Write your new word in the right-hand column.
  Check your spellings in a dictionary to see
  if you were correct.

purr	
call	
hiss	
live	
time	
whistle	
clap	
plan	
stop	

PHOTOCOPIABLE

Dear Helper,

Objective: to investigate and learn spellings of verbs (action words) with *-ed* and *-d* endings.

Using the explanation preceding the activity, help your child to describe what is happening to the original word when adding *-ed* and *-d*. Then, support your child with the activity, helping them to access a dictionary in order to check the spellings.

Name:

Match words to pictures

- Look at what the people are doing in the pictures and choose the word, from the list below, that matches the picture.
  Write the word underneath the picture.

clapping waving digging hopping building planting

- Write a sentence for each word.

1 ______________________________

2 ______________________________

3 ______________________________

4 ______________________________

5 ______________________________

6 ______________________________

Dear Helper,

Objective: to investigate and learn to spell words ending in *-ing*.

Your child will need most help when writing a sentence containing a word from the list. Discuss how the words might relate to personal experiences (eg mum and dad building a new garage, or planting a tree at school etc.).

W Name:

Spell well (4)

Remember!
Look at the word carefully.
Say the word aloud.
Cover the word while
you try to **write** the word.
Now **check** to see if it is right.

Look and Say	Cover	Write	Check
could			
should			
what			
where			
would			

Dear Helper,

Objective: to learn to spell common irregular words.

Help your child to spell these words by looking carefully at the letters in the word and saying the word aloud. Then fold the paper so that the word is covered. Encourage them to try and write the word. They should check their writing against the printed word. Lastly, make up sentences using the word. If your child uses the word as part of a question, remind them to use the question mark.

Name:

W

Missing vowels

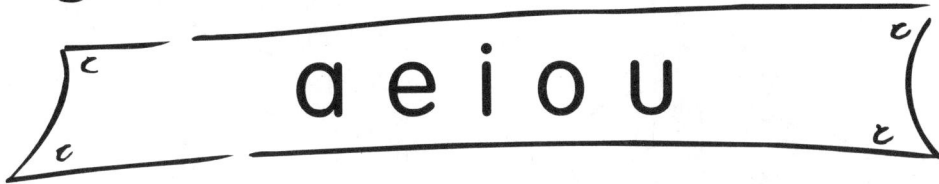

a e i o u

- Only the consonants are given for these words.
  Fill in the missing vowels.

b___ck___t

p___dd___ng

d___sh___s

p___ck___t

s___nb___d

r___ck___t

ch___stn___ts

p___cn___c

f___sh___ng

Dear Helper,

Objective: to know and use the terms 'vowel' and 'consonant'.

Help your child to decide what short sounding vowel to choose in order to complete the word. Use the terms *vowel* and *consonant* when talking about the letters.

PHOTOCOPIABLE

Name:

Jumbled words

- Put the words in these sentences in the right order, remembering that a sentence starts with a capital letter and ends with a full stop.
Write your sentences on the lines underneath.

riding bikes. are Two boys

eating ice cream. an is girl A

dog The is the chasing cat.

old walking An is his dog. man

feeding chicks. her The is bird

newspapers. A man selling is

PHOTOCOPIABLE

Dear Helper,

Objective: to re-order words to make sense.
Support your child by discussing all the things that are happening in the picture. Then, help to sort out the words into the right order. Remind your child about starting sentences with capital letters and ending with full stops.

Name:

S

Ill in bed

- The poem below is jumbled up.
  Write it in the correct order so it makes sense.

Hint: Use the rhymes at the end of the lines to help you find the right order.

She gave me orange through a straw

One day when I was ill in bed

I couldn't draw, I could only look

And asked me if I'd like to draw

At pictures in my favourite book

My mother came and felt my head

Write the poem here:

Dear Helper,

Objective: to re-order the sentences so that the poem makes sense.

Help your child to read each line. Ask: *Which is the most likely line to begin the poem?* Point out the rhyme endings to help your child sort the sentences into the right order.

Name:

Capital letters

- Re-write the sentences with capital letters in the correct places.

mr and mrs bean are welcome to visit
the school on thursday 17th of june.

at assembly on wednesday christine smedley
read the poem cats by eleanor farjeon.

several children chose books by roald dahl
to take home to read.

a favourite children's book is dogger
by shirley hughes.

Write your sentences here:

Dear Helper,

Objective: to use capital letters appropriately.

Help your child to read the sentences, making decisions together about where to put capital letters. Encourage and support your child in writing the sentences with the capital letters in the correct place. Talk about what capital letters are used for – beginning of sentences, names, book and poem titles, days of the week, months etc.

Name:

Sentences to punctuate

- Punctuate the following sentences using capital letters, full stops and question marks correctly.
  The first one has been done for you.

where were charlotte and emily going
Where were Charlotte and Emily going?

they were going to the fair

what can you do at a fair

charlotte can throw hoops

emily can roll pennies

why does charlotte want to throw hoops

charlotte wants to win a furry teddy

why does emily want to roll pennies

emily wants to win a goldfish

what else can you do at the fair

at the fair you can eat candy floss and go on rides

Dear Helper,

Objective: to punctuate sentences appropriately.

Help your child to read the sentences. Use the word *sentence* when talking about how to punctuate it correctly. When the task is complete, ask your child to read the sentences aloud using expression appropriate to the grammar, for example raising the voice for questions.

Name:

What is Dad thinking?

- The picture shows some of the things Dad likes doing.
- Write five sentences describing what he likes.
  Use the pictures to help you.

Write your sentences here:

Dear Helper,

Objective: to use information from the pictures to write in sentences to describe what Dad is thinking.

Talk to your child about the things Dad is thinking as he irons, and help your child to write five sentences about Dad's thoughts. The space in which to write the sentence is unlined so that your child knows a sentence can continue beyond the edge of the page by writing underneath. It is important that your child does not associate one line with one sentence.

PHOTOCOPIABLE

Name:

Question or not?

- Read the following sentences.
- Put a question mark at the end of the sentence if you think it is a question and a full stop at the end of those which are not.

Monkeys are mischievous

Are monkeys mischievous

What do pandas eat

Pandas eat bamboo plants

A tiger's coat is yellow and black striped

What colour is a tiger's coat

Polar bears can catch fish to eat

What do polar bears eat

Where do giraffes live

Giraffes live in Africa

Dear Helper,

Objective: to be able to identify questions and use the question mark appropriately.

Help your child to read each sentence and decide whether it is a question or not. You could help your child by reading the sentences aloud, using the expression and inflection appropriate to the ones that are questions.

Name:

The Bear's Just Had Twins!

- Fill in the missing rhyming words using this list:

day **said** **twins** **eat**
see **too** **mood**

The Bear's Just Had Twins!

Skipping and hopping we went to the zoo
With mummy and daddy and baby came ______________.
We whistled and sang as we went on our way,
All looking forward to a beautiful ______________.
The sun in the sky shone bright overhead,
And, once at the gate, the zookeeper ______________,
'Beware of the monkeys. They're throwing their food.
They woke up this morning in a mischievous ______________.
Please keep to the paths and put litter in bins.
Don't rattle the cages. The bear's just had ______________!'
'The bear's just had twins!', we all shouted with glee,
And briskly walked on so that we could ______________
The two little bears all cuddly and sweet
Meowing like kittens wanting something to ______________.

Kathleen Taylor

PHOTOCOPIABLE

Dear Helper,

Objective: to be able to predict the rhyming endings.

Read the poem with expression for your child, pausing at the appropriate point in order that your child can supply the missing rhyming word.

Name:

T

The Polar Bear and the Hobyahs

- Read the story.
- Then, re-tell it to your helper, making sure that you remember all that happens in the story.

Once upon a time there was a little old man and a little old woman who lived in a little house in the forest. They were very happy except at Christmas, because every Christmas the Hobyahs came.

The Hobyahs were very naughty, horrible little creatures who ate all the Christmas food, smashed all the Christmas presents and tore up all the Christmas cards every year.

One year, just before Christmas, a great big furry Polar Bear knocked at the door. 'Can I come in and stay for Christmas?' he asked. 'I'm very lonely and cold,' he said. The little old man and the little old woman felt very sorry for him so they let him in.

Then on Christmas Eve the Hobyahs came. They came down the chimney and in through the windows. They screeched and screamed as they ran all over the table and the shelves, smashing jars, eating food, spilling drink and lapping it up. They smashed presents and tore up cards, and then they sat on the Polar Bear because they thought he was a rug.

The Polar Bear did not like what the Hobyahs had done and, most of all, he didn't like them sitting on him. All of a sudden he roared and shook so that the Hobyahs fell on the floor and against the walls. The terrified Hobyahs ran out of the house while the Polar Bear still roared.

When they had all gone, the Polar Bear went over to the cupboard where the little old man and the little old woman were hiding and said, 'You can come out now.'

The little old woman said, 'Thank you' and gave the Polar Bear some warm milk. Then they all worked together to tidy the house and prepare the food for Christmas.

All was quiet and peaceful. As for the Hobyahs they were too frightened ever to return again.

Traditional story

Dear Helper,

Objective: to re-tell the story, giving the main points in sequence and to use appropriate expression.
Your child will need help in reading the story, so first read the story to your child. Then, read it again with your child joining in, in order to help your child remember the story. Then, listen to your child re-tell the story.

Name:

What happens next?

- Look at the pictures from the *Three Little Pigs* and *The Three Billy Goats Gruff* and write about what happens next.

Write what happens next:

Write what happens next:

Dear Helper,

Objective: to re-tell the story in order to discuss and write about what happens next.

Encourage your child to re-tell the stories of the two familiar traditional tales. Discuss the part of the story depicted in the pictures in order to help your child write what happens next.

PHOTOCOPIABLE

Name:

T

What sort of story?

- Read the blurbs on the backs of the books and discuss with your helper what you think the stories will be about.

Class 1 are very lucky to have a school cat who likes nothing better than to snuggle down on the cushions in their book corner. But is the school cat just a cat? Katie is sure she hears him say "Thank you" when she gives him a saucer of milk.
Daisy and Lucy are friends. Most of the time they get on very well, but when a new girl joins their class, their friendship becomes threatened.
Charlie is in a hurry to tell his mum about his part in a school play, but on the way home he meets some strange creatures.
Sarah goes to stay for a holiday with her grand-parents who live in a big house. She thinks she will be on her own with only Grandma and Grandad to play with. Then Tom arrives. From then on her days become very exciting!

Dear Helper,

Objective: to use book 'blurbs' in order to predict the content of the stories.

Help your child to read the book blurbs, one at a time, and discuss what the story might be about.

Name:

What's happening?

- Look at what is happening in the pictures and talk about it with your helper.
- Re-tell the story to your helper.
- Write what is happening in the picture in the space underneath each picture.

Dear Helper,

Objective: to say what is happening in the pictures and to re-tell the story.

Encourage your child to discuss what is happening in the pictures. Talk about the whole story of *Cinderella* and help your child to re-tell it. Support your child by helping them write a sentence about what is happening in each picture.

Name:

T

Tell a story, write a story

- The picture of children playing in the playground will be familiar to you. Think about things that have happened in your playground and tell the story to your helper.
- Ask your helper to help you write the story in the space underneath the picture.

Write your story here:

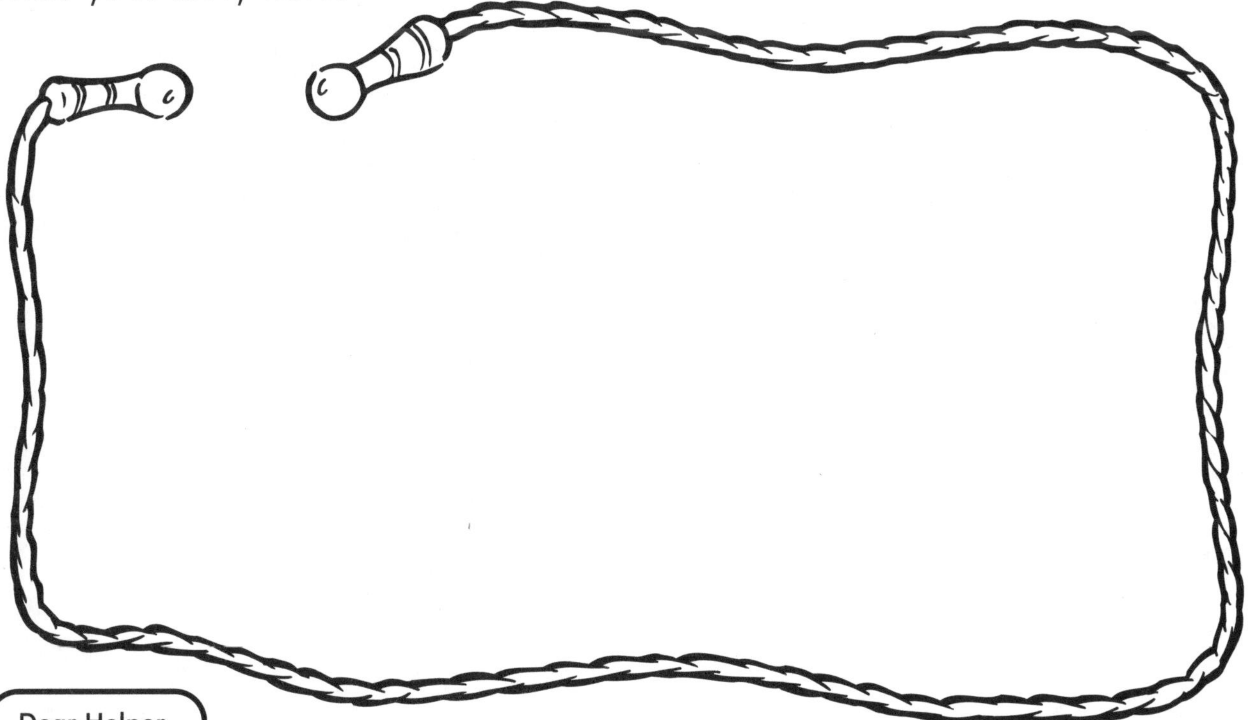

Dear Helper,

Objective: to write a story using a familiar setting.

Encourage your child to tell you about things that have happened during playtime, using the picture as a stimulus for ideas if necessary. Translating what is said into writing is difficult and your child will need you to help them to compose the story.

Name:

Create a poem

- Choose something you can see through the window at home. It could be something large, like the lawn. Or it could be something not so large, like a car. Or it could be something quite small, like a stone.
- Follow the model and examples below to compose your own poem.
- Think carefully about the best words to use in order to provide a word picture of what it is you have chosen.

	Poem 1	Poem 2
What is it? (one or two words)	the tulip	my pedal car
Where is it? (a few words)	on a straight stalk	where I left it
What is it doing? (one word)	glows	waiting.

Write your poem here:

What is it? ____________________

Where is it? ____________________

What is it doing? ____________________

Dear Helper,

Objective: to compose a poem using carefully selected words to form a picture.

Help your child with this task of composing a poem by talking about what can be seen through a window at home. Describe what can be seen, but focus on one thing to which your child is particularly drawn. Write down the things your child says about the subject, then help your child select the best words to use in the poem.

Name:

T

Create an animal poem

- Choose a creature. It can be one you like very much, or one that you don't like.
- Write three things about it, using one word for each thing. Each word must begin with the same letter – like this:

What (or who) are they?	caterpillars
What do they do?	crawl
How do they do this?	creepily

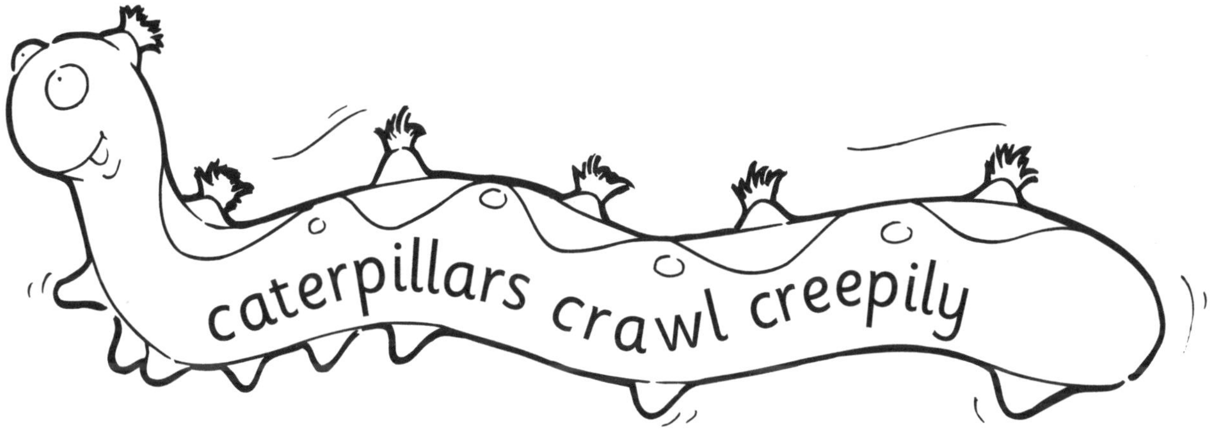
caterpillars crawl creepily

- Now you try:

What (or who) are they? ______________________________

What do they do? ______________________________

How do they do this? ______________________________

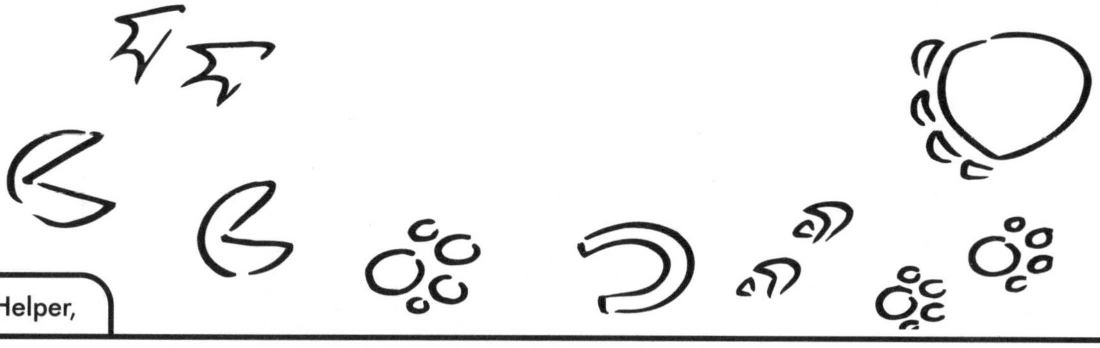

Dear Helper,

Objective: to compose a poem that has a poetic quality.

Help your child by discussing the creature they chose, building a range of words to choose from and use when composing their own poem.

PHOTOCOPIABLE

Name:

Sequence

Next you brush your teeth.

Now you go to bed.

To begin with you put toothpaste on your toothbrush.

After that you rinse your brush.

Finally you put the top back on the toothpaste.

Then you rinse your mouth with water.

- Cut out the sentences.
- Paste them onto a separate sheet in the correct order.

Dear Helper,

Objective: to re-order the sentences into the correct sequence.

Discuss with your child what you do when you brush your teeth. Talk about the order in which you do things, then read the sentences and help your child to sequence them into the correct order.

Name:

T

Favourite animals

The chart shows how some school children recorded a vote for their favourite animal.

			Yvonne	
			Kerry	Marie
Arthur			Robert	John
Joe	Tony	Angela	Katie	James
Sarah	Sam	Gemma	David	Sasha
polar bear	**monkey**	**tiger**	**panda**	**giraffe**

- Use the chart to help you answer the questions below. Part of the answer is written for you. Fill in the rest.

Which animal does Sam like the best?
Sam likes ______________ the best.

How many children like monkeys the best?
______________ children like monkeys the best.

Which animal is the most popular?
______________ is the most popular animal.

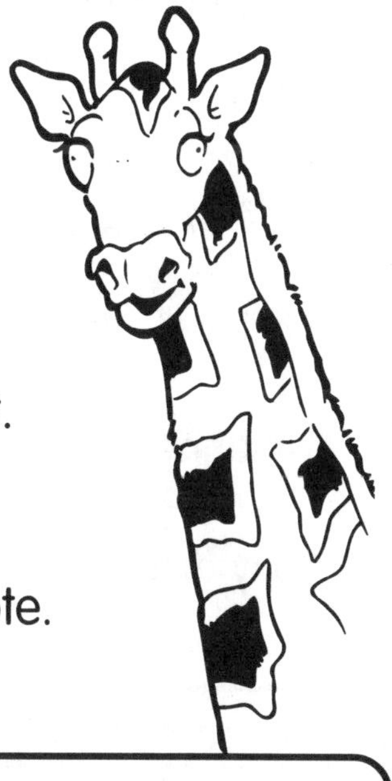

How many children voted altogether?
Altogether ______________ children voted.

Who liked the polar bear the best?
______________________________ polar bears the best.

Which two animals got the same vote?
______________ and ______________ got the same vote.

Dear Helper,

Objective: to be able to locate information on the chart in order to answer questions.
Support your child by helping them to read the questions and locate the information in order to write the answers.

T

Name:

My dad

- Look at this chart about dads.
- Use it to help you complete the sentences.

children's names	**Gemma**	**Zoran**	**Fredrick**	**Natasha**	**Tim**
What is dad's job?	engineer	looks after children	drives a lorry	works at the computer	looks after the house and children
Where does he work?	office	school	on the roads	at home	at home
What does he like doing?	bird watching	golf	fishing	walking	playing basketball
What is his favourite food?	lasagne	chicken chow mein	spare ribs	salmon	strawberries
What is he called?	Jim	Boris	Tony	Josh	Jeremy

1. Zoran's dad looks after ____________ in ____________ .

2. The dad who likes strawberries is called ____________ .

3. Natasha's dad works at the ____________ and likes ____________ and eating ____________ .

4. Tim's dad looks after ____________ at ____________.
   He likes playing ____________ and eating ____________.

5. Jeremy is ____________ dad. He works at ____________.

6. Golf is the favourite thing that ____________'s dad likes doing.

7. Lasagne is ____________ favourite food.

8. Tony drives ____________ and is ____________ dad.

Dear Helper,

Objective: to locate information on a chart.
Help your child to locate the information on the chart in order to complete the sentences.

Name:

T

My day at school

- Use the writing frame to help you write about your day at school.

This morning I went to school

To begin with

Next I

Then

After that

Finally I

Now

Dear Helper,

Objective: to be able to write an ordered sequence of events about the school day.

Discuss with your child the things that have happened at school. Then, using the writing frame, help your child to write about them in the sequence in which they occurred.

Name:

What I know about my mum

- Write eight things you know about your mum, for example:
  - What does she like?
  - What doesn't she like?
  - What's her favourite sport?
  - What's her favourite food?
  - What makes her so special?

Examples might be: Mum likes football.
She's kind.

- Then draw a picture of your mum in the frame.

Dear Helper,

Objective: to use the language and features of information text by providing short phrases or sentences to accompany a picture.

This is an opportunity for your child to talk freely and with confidence about someone who they know best. Help your child to capture the knowledge and thoughts they have about their mum in short phrases or sentences written around the picture.

Name:

T

Ask a question

- Write five questions you would like answered about the duck. Use the **question words** to start your questions.

  An example could be : Where do ducks sleep?

Don't forget the question mark!

Where

What

When

How

Why

Dear Helper,

Objective: to be able to write own questions.

Talk to your child about the duck in the picture and raise questions together. It is important for your child to be able to ask questions so they can look for their answers when reading. The question words *where, what, when, how and why* will help them to do this.

PHOTOCOPIABLE

Year 1 Homework Diary

Name ______________________________

Name of activity & date sent home	Helper's comments	Child's comments		Teacher's comments
		Did you like this? Draw a face. ☺ a lot ☹ a little ☹ not much	**How much did you learn?** Draw a face. ☺ a lot ☹ a little ☹ not much	